D1583253

Astrophel and Stella

SIR PHILIP SIDNEY

SIR PHILIP SIDNEY

Astrophel and Stella

Edited with an Introduction by
KINGSLEY HART

The Folio Society
London 1959

Printed in Great Britain by Western Printing Services Ltd, Bristol
Set in Poliphilus and Blado types
Bound by Webb Son & Co Ltd, London
Engraved frontispiece by Peter Reddick

Contents

5

Introduction

'BUT the truth is, his end was not writing, even while he wrote, nor his knowledge moulded for tables or schools, but both his wit and understanding bent upon his heart, to make himself and others, not in words or opinion, but in life and action, good and great.'

So wrote Sidney's life-long friend and biographer, Fulke Greville, and it is as a man of action and as a personality exerting a considerable influence upon his contemporaries that the impassioned lover of *Astrophel and Stella* is to be remembered, and not only as a man of letters. This is not to underestimate his contribution to English literature, which was both varied and influential: following in the steps of Surrey and Wyatt, he popularised the sonnet form and pro-duced a sonnet sequence second only to that of Shakespeare; with *The Defence of Poesie* he made a vital contribution to the development of literary criticism, and with the *Arcadia* started a fashion in prose romance.

But Greville, writing some twenty-five years after Sidney's death, was not the first to sing the praises of a man who was the embodiment of all Renaissance virtues. Princes, soldiers, diplomats, scholars, poets and divines are among those who, during his lifetime and immediately after his death at the age of thirty-two, extolled his moral and physical courage, his sincerity, his intellectual accomplishments, his skill as a diplomat, his physical beauty and his loyalty to his friends. But it is Greville again who provides the feature that unifies this great diversity of appreciation when he speaks of Sidney's concern for the Protestant cause: 'he made the religion he professed the firm basis of his life.' Catholic and Protestant, Spaniard and Dutchman, friend and enemy alike, pay tribute to the zeal and integrity with which he pursued his

7

belief in the rightness of the reformed religion. The accounts of his death on the field of battle seem more fitting to a saint than to a soldier, poet and statesman.

Philip Sidney was born in 1554. His father, Sir Henry Sidney, had held minor offices under Henry VIII, Edward VI and Mary. His mother was the daughter of the Duke of Northumberland, whose attempt to place Lady Jane Grey on the throne had cost him his life. In 1560 Sir Henry was appointed Lord President of the Marches of Wales, and the family went into residence at Ludlow Castle. From here Philip was sent to Shrewsbury Grammar School, where he began his formal education on the same day as Fulke Greville. Greville's picture of the schoolboy Philip is thus an authoritative one:

'. . . though I lived with him, and knew him from a child, yet I never knew him other than a man: with such staidness of mind, lovely and familiar gravity, as carried grace and reverence above greater years. His talk ever of knowledge, and his very play tending to enrich his mind, so as his teachers found something in him to observe, and learn, above that which they had usually read or taught. Which eminence by nature, and industry, made his worthy Father title Sir Philip in my hearing (though I unseen) *Lumen familiae suae.*'

Later, at Oxford, where Philip entered Christ Church in 1568, Sir William Cecil (afterwards Lord Burghley) wrote to Sir Henry: 'increase of all goodness to your son, my darling master Philip. He is worthy to be loved, as so I do love him as he were my son.' However, a proposal by Sir Henry that a marriage should be arranged between Philip and Cecil's daughter, Anne, was received rather coolly. Anne later made a more profitable match with the young Earl of Oxford. Sidney and Oxford were destined to meet under dramatic circumstances in 1581, when as a result of a political quarrel on the tennis court, Sidney challenged Oxford to a duel, fortunately prevented by the Council.

Sidney left Oxford without taking a degree. His education for the career ahead of him as a man of affairs was continued in the form of continental travel. Early in 1572 he received a licence from Queen Elizabeth 'to go out of England into parts beyond the seas for two years for his attaining the knowledge of foreign languages.' In Paris, where he came under the protection of Sir Francis Walsingham, he was present at the massacre of St Bartholomew's Eve. This strengthened his sympathy for the Protestant cause, and provided him with an experience that he was never to forget in his attempts to establish a Protestant League in Europe. Here, too, he probably met the scholar and diplomat, Hubert Languet, whom he joined later in Frankfurt and Vienna. Languet, an envoy of the Elector of Saxony, was one of the most important Huguenot leaders, and his friendship with Sidney was one of the most significant single influences on Sidney's early life and became a deep and lasting one. They corresponded for many years, and Sidney's 'grand tour' was largely planned on Languet's advice. It was to include Heidelberg, Strasbourg, Hungary, Poland and Italy, and when Sidney returned to England in 1575, he had acquired a knowledge of continental politics and personalities that was to stand him in good stead on future official missions.

In 1576, after a short period at court, Sidney joined his father in Ireland, where Sir Henry was Lord Deputy. Philip was no passive observer of the disturbances there, but an active supporter of his father's policy, which was not entirely approved of in London. In the following year we find the first of many examples of Sidney's outspoken sincerity and moral integrity in political matters in his *Discourse on Ireland*, which he doubtless realised would not gain him the Queen's enthusiastic support.

The visit to Ireland introduces one of the few direct links between Sidney and Penelope Devereux, the Stella of the sonnets. Penelope's father, the first Earl of Essex, who had taken an interest in Philip ever since his schooldays, was taking part in the campaign in Ulster. Essex was suddenly stricken with a fatal illness, and Sidney arrived too late in response to his urgent summons. Essex had, however, left this testimony:

'Tell him I send him nothing, but I wish him well, and so well that if God do move both their hearts I wish that he might match with my daughter. I call him son; he is so wise, so virtuous and godly; and if he go on in the course he hath begun, he will be as famous and worthy a gentleman as ever England had.'

Philip had almost certainly met Penelope by then, as she would have been present when her mother entertained the Queen at Chartley Castle during the Royal Progress the year before, when the Sidney family formed part of the Queen's retinue. Essex's secretary seemed most anxious to pursue the matter, for he wrote to Sir Henry:

'Truly my Lord, I must say to your Lordship, as I have said to my Lord of Leicester and Mr Philip, the breaking off from this match, if the fault be on your parts, will turn to more dishonour than can be repaired with any other marriage in England.'

There is no record that either father or son showed any interest in acting further in the matter, and the names of Philip and Penelope are nowhere else found linked in correspondence.

In 1577 Philip began to follow the course prophesied for him by the dying Essex. In February of that year he was sent as the Queen's accredited envoy to the Emperor Rudolph to convey her condolences to him on the death of his father. In the space of a few months Sidney succeeded in enhancing his reputation considerably, winning the praises of Don John of Austria (Governor of the Netherlands) and Prince William of Orange, who said that Sidney only lacked the opportunity to become one of the greatest statesmen in Europe. Walsingham wrote to Sir Henry: 'There hath not been any gentleman, I am sure, these many years, that hath gone through so honourable a charge with as great commendations as he.' Sidney's aim in visiting Prince William had been to gain his interest in the formation of a Protestant League. The Queen, who was not anxious to support such a scheme, must have realised this, for despite Sidney's obvious success as a diplomat, he was given no further commission for some time. Her reluctance to employ him must have been strengthened by the outspokenness and sincerity of the Memorial which he addressed to her in 1579, at the instigation of Leicester and Walsingham, stating the objections to her proposed marriage to the Duke of Anjou. A man of whom Greville could write 'his heart and tongue went both one way, and so with every one that went with the truth', was not likely to find special favour at Elizabeth's court. Indeed, she appears to have been one of the few who was not affected by Sidney's personal magnetism, which would explain the difficulty he had in the years that followed in gaining preferment at court.

During 1579 Sidney began to spend a great deal of time away from the court. His friendship with the poet Spenser, to whom he gave considerable encouragement, was cemented, and when *The Shepherd's Calendar* appeared in 1579 it was dedicated to him. Some of his time was spent with his sister, the Countess of Pembroke, at Wilton. It was here that the first version of the *Arcadia*, written for her, was completed. Here, too, he began his *Defence of Poesie* as a reply to the Puritan attack on poetry by Stephen Gosson in *The School of Abuse*, also published in 1579. For Sidney's literary activity the importance of the close companionship and critical encouragement of his sister cannot be exaggerated. On some enterprises they worked together, and it was the intimate knowledge of his work that gave such authority to the Countess's preparation of the 1598 folio. But as Greville said, 'he purposed no monuments of books to the world', and this literary activity must have been accompanied by a certain amount of impatience at his lack of advancement at court.

In 1581, however, he became a Member of Parliament, and the part he played in public life increased steadily until his death. He was given a subordinate position under his uncle the Earl of Warwick, Master of the Ordinance, and in 1585 he was made Joint Master.

In January, 1583, he was knighted. Not on account of his own achievements, but in order that he might stand proxy for the Elector Casimir at an installation of Garter Knights at Windsor. In the 1584 Parliament he was active in committee work, particularly in connection with the letters patent granted to Walter Raleigh for land in Virginia. This brought him into close contact with Drake and encouraged the interest in exploration and discovery, typical of the Renaissance mind, which he had already shown in dealings with the Cathay Company in 1577. Sidney himself aspired to be general of the land forces in Drake's expedition to the West Indies, and he had even joined Drake at Plymouth in August 1585, but was suddenly summoned to London to learn that he had been appointed Governor of Flushing. He achieved immediate popularity in the Low Countries, and his death in action in the following year during Leicester's campaign was felt as strongly by the Dutch as it was in England. Formal expressions of grief and eulogies of praise, ranging from the latin verses of the University of Cambridge to the incongruity of Spenser's pastoral lament, a state funeral, the wish of the States of Zeeland to raise a monument to him in gold, are a measure of the extent to which his loss was felt. The most expressive tribute, however, was that of his friend, Greville:

'Indeed he was a true model of worth; a man fit for conquest, plantation, reformation, or what action soever is greatest and hardest amongst men. Withall, such a lover of mankind, and goodness, that whosoever had any real parts, in him found comfort, participation and protection to the uttermost of his power; like *Zephyrus* he giving life where he blew.'

The history of *Astrophel and Stella* is strangely detached from the short but rich life outlined above, and the actual degree of contact which took place between Sidney and Penelope Devereux is difficult to establish. It has been seen that her father, the Earl of Essex, suggested

12

a marriage in 1576 when Penelope was barely fourteen, but that no action was taken by the Sidneys. The possibility of closer contact might have existed after the widowed Countess of Essex married the Earl of Leicester two years later. Sidney certainly met Penelope in 1575, probably also at Wilton some years later as his sister's guest, and possibly both at the Countess of Leicester's home at Wanstead and at court. But facts are more important than conjectured meetings. By 1581 Penelope was secretly betrothed to Charles Blount, but her guardians ignored this and engineered a marriage for her with Lord Rich. The exact date of the marriage is not known, but was probably sometime in the first half of 1581, and knowledge of its imminent approach may have reached Sidney earlier. The marriage was an unhappy one, but it should not be supposed that it was because Penelope was eating her heart out for Sidney. Lord Rich divorced her in 1605, whereupon she promptly married her childhood sweet-heart Blount, who had become the Earl of Devonshire. References to Sidney's own proposed marriage to Frances Walsingham can be found as early as December 1581. They were married in September 1583, and there is no reason to suppose that this marriage was anything but a successful one.

The sonnets and songs of *Astrophel and Stella* may, then, have been written between 1578 and 1583. It seems unlikely that they would have occupied Sidney before he started upon the *Arcadia* in 1577, and even more unlikely that he would have continued them after his own marriage. What is quite certain, however, is that on the internal evidence of the poems themselves he did continue to address Penelope after her marriage to Lord Rich.

The sequence falls into two clear though unequal divisions: Sonnets 1-32, and Sonnet 33 to the end. The Astrophel of the earlier sonnets seems to have more in common with the Philisides of the incidental poetry of the *Arcadia*. He is more concerned with Stella's physical attractions than with his own uncontrollable passions. Indeed, the set of verses in the *Arcadia* addressed to Mira might well

13

be regarded as Astrophel's first addresses to Stella, together with the first group of sonnets representing the slow awakening of Sidney's feelings for Penelope. Sidney himself stresses retrospectively the gradual nature of the growth of his feelings in Sonnet 2. Some of the early sonnets show, too, a concern for literary matters, and can be associated with the discussions in the *Defence of Poesie*. In Sonnets 3, 6 and 15, Sidney seems to be more concerned with giving expression to his ideas about poetry in general than with his real feelings for Stella. With Sonnet 33 the whole tone of the sequence changes. Whereas it might be possible to accuse Sidney of indulging in a conventional form of literary expression in the early sonnets, the later ones give ample proof of the sincerity of his feelings for Penelope. It is this particular quality, so strong a feature in the man himself, which makes him a poet, and raises the whole sequence to a much higher level of achievement than the work of many of his contemporaries.

There can be little doubt that the order of the sonnets as we have them was fixed by Sidney himself, but there is no evidence that he arranged them in any particular chronological order. After Sonnet 86 there seems to be some lack of continuity, and the particular tone of these last sonnets and the eleventh song would suggest that they were written at intervals after the main group and not completely revised by Sidney himself. Certain sonnets contain particular references which help to fix their dates reasonably accurately. The historical references in Sonnet 30 suggest that it was composed early in 1581; Sonnet 41 suggests that Stella was an observer at the tourney held to entertain the French Commissioners in April 1581, in which Sidney himself took part.

On the whole, the internal evidence of the sonnets would suggest that Sidney's consuming passion for Penelope was short lived. Slow in awakening, it suddenly assumed a passionate intensity after Sonnet 32, reflected not only in the despair of his sufferings but also in the jealous invective of Sonnet 37, clearly aimed at Lord Rich after Penelope's marriage. This particular sonnet was restored to the

14

sequence by the Countess of Pembroke in the 1598 folio. The sustained nature of the feeling throughout the sequence between Sonnets 33 and 86 suggests that this central section was written over a period of a few months, probably just after Penelope's marriage, and that during this time Sidney and Penelope met, and the exchanges described in some of the later sonnets and songs in this group actually took place. It is difficult to substantiate such a theory, but on the other hand there is even less reason to suppose, as earlier editors did, that the carrying on of a clandestine affair with a married woman was a criminal offence that a man of Sidney's integrity would not have committed. On the contrary, the spirit in which Sidney would have entered into such an exchange is entirely in keeping with the spirit of the age in which he lived.

The sonnets were circulated in manuscript during Sidney's lifetime, with the probable exception of those referring to Lord Rich, numbers 24 and 37. There are therefore manifold textual problems arising from the three unauthorised editions printed from such manuscripts before the folio of 1598, owing to the vagaries of Elizabethan copyists and the lack of imagination revealed by the unauthorised printers in deciphering bad manuscripts.

The present edition follows the practice of most modern editions of Sidney's works in using the 1598 folio. In certain places readings have been taken from one of the quartos or in a few instances from one of the surviving manuscripts. These variants have been adopted where they assist the modern reader to understand Sidney's thought more readily, but only where there has been sufficient authority for doing so. Spelling and punctuation have been modernised, although certain Elizabethan forms have been retained to conform with the metrical demands of the poetry.

KINGSLEY HART

15

 *1*

Loving in truth and fain in verse my love to show,
That she, dear she, might take some pleasure of my pain—
Pleasure might cause her read, reading might make her
    know,
Knowledge might pity win, and pity grace obtain—
I sought fit words to paint the blackest face of woe,
Studying inventions fine, her wits to entertain,
Oft turning others' leaves, to see if thence would flow
Some fresh and fruitful showers upon my sun-burn'd
    brain.
But words came halting forth, wanting invention's stay;
Invention, Nature's child, fled stepdame Study's blows,
And others' feet still seem'd but strangers in my way.
Thus, great with child to speak, and helpless in my throes,
Biting my truant pen, beating myself for spite:
'Fool,' said my Muse to me, 'look in thy heart and write.'

2

Not at the first sight, nor with a dribbèd* shot,
Love gave the wound, which while I breath will bleed;
But known worth did in mine of time* proceed,
Till, by degrees, it had full conquest got.
I saw and lik'd; I lik'd but lovèd not;
I lov'd, but straight did not what Love decreed.
At length to Love's decrees I, forc'd, agreed,
Yet with repining at so partial lot.
Now even that footstep* of lost liberty
Is gone, and now, like slave-born Muscovite,
I call it praise to suffer tyranny,
And now employ the remnant of my wit
To make myself believe that all is well,
While with a feeling skill I paint my hell.

3

Let dainty wits cry on the Sisters nine,
That, bravely mask'd, their fancies may be told;
Or, Pindar's apes,★ flaunt they in phrases fine,
Enam'ling with pied flowers their thoughts of gold;
Or else let them in statelier glory shine,
Ennobling new-found tropes★ with problems old;
Or with strange similes enrich each line,
Of herbs or beasts which Ind or Afric hold.
For me, in sooth, no Muse but one I know;
Phrases and problems from my reach do grow,
And strange things cost too dear for my poor sprites.★
How then? Even thus: in Stella's *face I read*
What Love and Beauty be; then all my deed
But copying is, what in her, Nature writes.

4

Virtue, alas, now let me take some rest;
Thou set'st a bate* between my will and wit;
If vain love have my simple soul oppress'd,
Leave what thou lik'st not, deal not thou with it.
Thy sceptre use in some old Cato's breast,
Churches or schools are for thy seat more fit;
I do confess—pardon a fault confess'd—
My mouth too tender is for thy hard bit.
But if that needs thou wilt usurping be
The little reason that is left in me,
And still th'effect of thy persuasions prove,
I swear my heart such one shall show to thee,
That shrines in flesh so true a deity,
That, Virtue, thou thyself shalt be in love.

5

It is most true that eyes are form'd to serve
The inward light, and that the heavenly part
Ought to be a king, from whose rules who do swerve,
Rebels to nature, strive for their own smart.
It is most true, what we call Cupid's dart
An image is, which for ourselves we carve,
And, fools, adore in temple of our heart,
Till that good god make church and churchman starve.
True that true beauty virtue is indeed,
Whereof this beauty can be but a shade*
Which elements with mortal mixture breed;
True that on earth we are but pilgrims made,
And should in soul up to our country* move:
True, and yet true that I must Stella love.

 6

Some lovers speak, when they their Muses entertain,
Of hopes begot by fear, of wot not what desires,
Of force of heavenly beams infusing hellish pain,
Of living deaths, dear wounds, fair storms and freezing
    fires;
Some one his song in Jove and Jove's strange tales attires,
Border'd with bulls and swans, powder'd with golden rain;
Another humbler wit* to shepherd's pipe retires,
Yet hiding royal blood full oft in rural vein.
To some a sweetest plaint a sweetest style affords,
While tears pour out his ink, and sighs breathe out his
    words,
His paper pale despair, and pain his pen doth move.
I can speak what I feel, and feel as much as they,
But think that all the map of my state I display
When trembling voice brings forth that I do Stella love.

7

When Nature made her chief work, Stella's eyes,
In colour black, why wrapp'd she beams so bright?
Would she in beamy black, like painter wise,
Frame daintiest lustre mix'd of shades and light?
Or did she else that sober hue devise,
In object best to knit and strength our sight,
Lest, if no veil those brave gleams did disguise,
They, sun-like, should more dazzle than delight?
Or would she her miraculous power show
That, whereas black seems Beauty's contrary,
She, even in black, doth make all beauties flow?
Both so, and thus: she, minding love should be
Plac'd ever there, gave him this mourning weed
To honour all their deaths who for her bleed.

8

Love, born in Greece, of late fled from his native place,
Forc'd, by a tedious proof, that Turkish-harden'd heart
Is no fit mark to pierce with his fine-pointed dart,*
And pleas'd with our soft peace, stay'd here his flying race.
But finding these north climes do coldly him embrace—
Not used to frozen clips*—he strove to find some part
Where with most ease and warmth he might employ his art.
At length he perch'd himself in Stella's joyful face,
Whose fair skin, beamy eyes, like morning sun on snow,
Deceiv'd the quaking boy, who thought from so pure light
Effects of lively heat must needs in nature grow.
But she most fair, most cold, made him thence take his
    flight
To my close heart, where, while some firebrands he did lay,
He burn'd unwares his wings, and cannot fly away.

9

Queen Virtue's Court, which some call Stella's face,
Prepar'd by Nature's choicest furniture,
Hath his front built of alabaster pure;
Gold is the covering of that stately place.
The door by which sometimes comes forth her grace,
Red porphir is, which lock of pearl makes sure,
Whose porches rich—which name of cheeks endure—
Marble mix'd red and white do interlace.
The windows now through which this heavenly guest
Looks o'er the world, and can find nothing such
Which dare claim from those lights the name of best,
Of touch* they are, that without touch doth touch,
Which Cupid's self from Beauty's mine did draw,
Of touch they are, and poor I am their straw.

10

Reason, in faith thou art well serv'd that still
Would'st brabbling* be with Sense and Love in me.
I rather wish'd thee climb the Muse's hill,
Or reach the fruit of Nature's choicest tree,
Or seek heaven's course, or heaven's inside to see:
Why should'st thou toil our thorny soil to till?
Leave Sense and those which Sense's objects be,
Deal thou with powers of thoughts, leave Love to Will.
But thou would'st needs fight both with Love and Sense,
With sword of wit, giving wounds of dispraise,
Till downright blows did foil thy cunning fence;
For soon as they struck thee with Stella's rays,
Reason, thou kneeld'st and offered'st straight to prove
By reason good, good reason her to love.

In truth, O Love, with what a boyish kind
Thou dost proceed in thy most serious ways,
That when the heaven to thee his best displays,
Yet of that best thou leav'st the best behind!
For, like a child that some fair book doth find,
With gilded leaves or colour'd vellum plays,
Or at the most on some fine picture stays,
But never heeds the fruit of writer's mind,
So when thou saw'st, in Nature's cabinet,
Stella, thou straight lookt'st babies* in her eyes,
In her cheeks' pit thou did'st thy pitfold* set,
And in her breast bo-peep or couching lies,*
Playing and shining in each outward part;
But, fool, seek'st not to get into her heart!

 *12*

Cupid, because thou shin'st in Stella's *eyes,*
That from her locks, thy day-nets,* none 'scapes free,
That those lips swell, so full of thee they be,
That her sweet breath makes oft thy flames to rise,
That in her breast thy pap well sugar'd lies,
That her grace gracious makes thy wrongs, that she,
What words soe'er she speak, persuades for thee,
That her clear voice lifts thy face to the skies—
Thou countest Stella *thine, like those whose powers*
Having got up a breach by fighting well,
Cry, 'Victory, this fair day all is ours!'
O no! Her heart is such a citadel,
So fortified with wit, stor'd with disdain,
That to win it is all the skill and pain.

13

Phoebus was judge between Jove, Mars and Love,
Of those three gods, whose arms the fairest were.
Jove's golden shield did eagle sables bear,
Whose talons held young Ganymede above;
But in vert* field Mars bore a golden spear
Which through a bleeding heart his point did shove;
Each had his crest, Mars carried Venus' glove,
Jove on his helm the thunderbolt did rear.
Cupid then smiles, for on his crest there lies
Stella's fair hair, her face he makes his shield,
Where roses gules* are borne in silver field.
Phoebus drew wide the curtains of the skies
To blaze* these last, and swore devoutly then:
The first, thus match'd, were scantly gentlemen.

 14

Alas, have I not pain enough, my friend,
Upon whose breast a fiercer gripe doth tire*
Than did on him who first stole down the fire,
While Love on me doth all his quiver spend,
But with your rhubarb words* ye must contend
To grieve me worse, in saying that Desire
Doth plunge my well-form'd soul even in the mire
Of sinful thoughts, which do in ruin end?
If that be sin which doth the manners frame,
Well stay'd with truth in word and faith of deed,
Ready of wit, and fearing nought but shame,
If that be sin which in fix'd hearts doth breed
A loathing of all loose unchastity—
Then love is sin, and let me sinful be.

15

You that do search for every purling spring
Which from the ribs of old Parnassus flows,
And every flower, not sweet perhaps, which grows
Near thereabouts, into your poesy wring;
Ye that do dictionary's method bring
*Into your rhymes, running in rattling rows;**
You that poor Petrarch's long deceasèd woes
With new-born signs and denizen'd wit do sing:*
You take wrong ways; those far-fet helps be such*
*As do bewray a want of inward touch,**
And sure at length stol'n goods do come to light.
But if—both for your love and skill—your name
You seek to nurse at fullest breast of Fame,
Stella *behold, and then begin to indite.*

16

In nature apt to like when I did see
Beauties which were of many carats fine,
My boiling sprites did thither soon incline,
And, Love, I thought that I was full of thee.
But finding not those restless flames in me
Which others said did make their souls to pine,
I thought those babes of some pin's hurt did whine,
By my soul judging what Love's pain might be.
But while I thus with this young lion play'd,
Mine eyes—shall I say curst or blest?—beheld
Stella; now she is nam'd need more be said?
In her sight I a lesson new have spell'd:
I now have learn'd Love right, and learn'd e'en so
As they that being poison'd poison know.

His mother dear, Cupid offended late,
Because that Mars, grown slacker in her love,
With pricking shot he did not throughly move
To keep the pace of their first loving state.
The boy refus'd for fear of Mars's hate,
Who threaten'd stripes if he his wrath did prove;
But she, in chafe,* him from her lap did shove,
Brake bow, brake shafts, while Cupid weeping sat,
Till that his grandam Nature, pitying it,
Of Stella's brows made him two better bows,
And in her eyes of arrows infinite.
O how for joy he leaps! O how he crows!
And straight therewith, like wags new got to play,
Falls to shrewd turns; and I was in his way!

18

With what sharp checks I in myself am shent*
When into Reason's audit I do go,
And by just counts myself a bankrupt know
Of all those goods which heaven to me hath lent;
Unable quite to pay even Nature's rent,
Which unto it by birthright I do owe;
And, which is worse, no good excuse can show,
But that my wealth I have most idly spent!
My youth doth waste, my knowledge brings forth
    toys,*
My wit doth strive those passions to defend
Which, for reward, spoil it with vain annoys.
I see my course to lose myself doth bend;
I see, and yet no greater sorrow take
Than that I lose no more for Stella's sake.

19

On Cupid's bow how are my heart-strings bent,
That see my wrack and yet embrace the same!
When most I glory then I feel most shame;
I willing run, yet while I run repent;
My best wits still their own disgrace invent,
My very ink turns straight to Stella's name,
And yet my words, as them my pen doth frame,
Advise themselves that they are vainly spent.
For though she pass all things, yet what is all
That unto me, who fare like him that both
Looks to the skies and in a ditch doth fall?
O let me prop my mind, yet in his growth,
And not in nature for best fruits unfit:
'Scholar,' saith Love, 'bend hitherward your wit.'

Fly, fly, my friends! I have my death wound—fly!
See there that boy, that murd'ring boy, I say,
Who like a thief hid in dark bush doth lie,
Till bloody bullet get him wrongful prey.
So tyrant he no fitter place could spy,
Nor so fair level in so secret stay,*
As that sweet black which veils the heavenly eye:
There himself with his shot he close doth lay.
Poor passenger, pass now thereby I did,
And stay'd, pleas'd with the prospect of the place,
While that black hue from me the bad guest hid;
But straight I saw motions of lightning grace,
And then descried the glistring of his dart:
But ere I could fly thence, it pierc'd my heart.

Your words, my friend—right healthful caustics—blame
My young mind marr'd, whom Love doth windlass* so,
That mine own writings, like bad servants, show
My wits quick in vain thoughts, in virtue lame;
That Plato I read for nought but if he tame
Such coltish gyres;* that to my birth I owe
Nobler desires, lest else that friendly foe,
Great expectation, wear a train of shame.
For since mad March great promise made of me,
If now the May of my years much decline,
What can be hoped my harvest time will be?
Sure, you say well, 'Your wisdom's golden mine
Dig deep with Learning's spade.' Now tell me this:
Hath this world aught so fair as Stella is?

 22

In highest way of heaven the sun did ride,
Progressing then from fair Twin's* golden place,
Having no scarf of clouds before his face,
But shining forth of heat in his chief pride,
When some fair ladies, by hard promise tied,
On horseback met him in his furious race;
Yet each prepar'd, with fans' well-shading grace,
From that foe's wounds their tender skins to hide.
Stella alone with face unarmèd march'd,
Either to do like him which open shone,
Or careless of the wealth, because her own.
Yet were the hid and meaner beauties parch'd,
Her daintiest bare went free. The cause was this:
The sun, which others burn'd, did her but kiss.

The curious wits, seeing dull pensiveness
Bewray* itself in my long-settled eyes,
Whence those same fumes of melancholy rise,
With idle pains and missing aim do guess.
Some, that know my spring I did address,
Deem that my Muse some fruit of knowledge plies;
Others, because the Prince my service tries,
Think that I think State errors to redress.
But harder judges judge ambition's rage,
Scourge of itself, still climbing slipp'ry place,
Holds my young brain captiv'd in golden cage.
O fools, or over-wise! Alas, the race
Of all my thoughts hath neither stop nor start,
But only Stella's eyes and Stella's heart.

24

Rich* fools there be whose base and filthy heart
Lies hatching still the goods wherein they flow,
And damning their own selves to Tantal's smart,*
Wealth breeding want, more rich, more wretched grow.
Yet to those fools Heaven doth such wit impart
As what their hands do hold, their heads do know,
And knowing love, and loving lay apart
As sacred things, far from all danger's show.
But that rich fool who by blind Fortune's lot
The richest gem of love and life enjoys,
And can with foul abuse such beauties blot,
Let him, depriv'd of sweet but unfelt joys,
Exil'd for aye from those high treasures which
He knows not, grow in only folly rich!

 25

The wisest scholar of the wight most wise
By Phoebus' doom,* with sugar'd sentence says
That virtue, if it once met with our eyes,
Strange flames of love it in our souls would raise.
But—for that man with pain this truth descries
Whiles he each thing in Sense's balance weighs,
And so, nor will nor can behold those skies
Which inward sun to heroic minds displays—
Virtue of late, with virtuous care to stir
Love of herself, took Stella's shape, that she
To mortal eyes might sweetly shine in her.
It is most true, for since I her did see,
Virtue's great beauty in that face I prove,
And find the effect—for I do burn in love.

Though dusty wits dare scorn Astrology,
And fools can think those lamps of purest light—
Whose numbers, ways, greatness, eternity,
Promising wonders, wonders do invite—
To have for no cause birthright in the sky
But for to spangle the black weeds of Night,
Or for some braule* which in that chamber high
They should still dance to please a gazer's sight:
For me, I do Nature unidle know,
And know great causes great effects procure,
And know those bodies high reign on the low.
And if these rules did fail, proof makes me sure
Who oft fore-judge my after-following race,
By only those two stars in Stella's face.

Because I oft in dark abstracted guise
Seem most alone in greatest company,
With dearth of words or answers quite awry,
To them that would make speech of speech arise,
They deem, and of their doom* the rumour flies,
That poison foul of bubbling pride doth lie
So in my swelling breast that only I
Fawn on myself, and others do despise.
Yet pride I think doth not my soul possess,
(Which looks too oft in his unflatt'ring glass)
But one worse fault, ambition, I confess,
That makes me oft my best friends overpass
Unseen, unheard, while thought to highest place
Bends all his powers, e'en unto Stella's grace.

You that with Allegory's curious frame
Of others' children changelings use to make,
With me those pains, for God's sake do not take:
I list not dig so deep for brazen fame.
When I say 'Stella', I do mean the same
Princess of beauty for whose only sake
The reins of Love I love, though never slake,*
And joy therein, though nations count it shame.
I beg no subject to use eloquence,
Nor in hid ways to guide philosophy;
Look at my hands for no such quintessence,
But know that I in pure simplicity
Breathe out the flames which burn within my heart,
Love only reading unto me this art.

Like some weak lords, neighbour'd by mighty kings,
To keep themselves and their chief cities free
Do easily yield that all their coasts may be
Ready to store their camps of needful things,
So Stella's heart, finding what power Love brings
To keep itself in life and liberty,
Doth willing grant that in the frontiers he
Use all to help his other conquerings.
And thus her heart escapes, but thus her eyes
Serve him with shot, her lips his heralds are,
Her breasts his tents, legs his triumphal car,
Her flesh his food, her skin his armour brave;
And I, but for because my prospect lies
Upon that coast, am given up for a slave.

Whether the Turkish new moon minded be
To fill his horns this year on Christian coast?
How Poles' right king means without leave of host
To warm with ill-made fire cold Muscovy?
If French can yet three parts in one agree?
What now the Dutch in their full diets boast?
How Holland hearts, now so good towns be lost,
Trust in the shade of pleasing Orange tree?
How Ulster likes of that same golden bit
Wherewith my father once made it half tame?
If in the Scottish Court be weltring* yet?
These questions busy wits to me do frame;
I, cumber'd with good manners, answer do,
But know not how: for still I think of you.

31

With how sad steps, O Moon, thou climb'st the skies!
How silently, and with how wan a face!
What, may it be that even in heavenly place
That busy archer his sharp arrows tries?
Sure, if that long-with-love-acquainted eyes
Can judge of love, thou feel'st a lover's case:
I read it in thy looks; thy languish'd grace,
To me that feel the like, thy state descries.
Then even of fellowship, O Moon, tell me
Is constant love deem'd there but want of wit?
Are beauties there as proud as here they be?
Do they above love to be lov'd, and yet
Those lovers scorn whom that love doth possess?
Do they call virtue there ungratefulness?

Morpheus, the lively son of deadly Sleep,
Witness of life to them that living die,
A prophet oft, and oft an history,
A poet eke, as humours fly or creep;
Since thou in me so sure a power dost keep,
That never I with clos'd-up sense do lie
But by thy work my Stella I descry,
Teaching blind eyes both how to smile and weep;
Vouchsafe of all acquaintance this to tell,
Whence hast thou ivory, rubies, pearl, and gold
To show her skin, lips, teeth, and head so well?
'Fool!' answers he, 'no Inds such treasures hold,
But from thy heart, while my sire charmeth thee,
Sweet Stella's image I do steal to me.'

I might—unhappy word!—O me, I might,
And then would not, or could not, see my bliss,
Till now wrapt in a most infernal night,
I found how heavenly day, wretch! I did miss.
Heart, rent thyself, thou dost thyself but right,
No lovely Paris made thy Helen his,
No force, no fraud robb'd thee of thy delight,
Nor Fortune of thy fortune author is,
But to myself myself did give the blow,
While too much wit, forsooth, so troubled me,
That I respects for both our sakes must show,
And yet could not by rising moon foresee
How fair a day was near; O punish'd eyes,
That I had been more foolish, or more wise!

34

'Come let me write.' 'And to what end?' 'To ease
A burthen'd heart.' 'How can words ease, which are
The glasses of thy daily vexing care?'
'Oft cruel fights well-pictures forth do please.'
'Art not asham'd to publish thy disease?'
'Nay, that may breed my fame, it is so rare.'
'But will not wise men think thy words fond ware?'
'Then be they close, and so none shall displease.'
'What idler thing than speak and not be heard?'
'What harder thing than smart and not to speak?'
'Peace, foolish wit! with wit my wit is marr'd.'
Thus write I, while I doubt to write, and wreak
My harms on ink's poor loss; perhaps some find
Stella's great powers that so confuse my mind.*

35

What may words say, or what may words not say
Where Truth itself must speak like Flattery?
Within what bounds can one his liking stay,
Where Nature doth with infinite agree?
What Nestor's counsel* can my flames allay,
Since Reason self doth blow the coal in me?
And, ah! what hope that Hope should once see day,
Where Cupid is sworn page to Chastity?
Honour is honour'd that thou dost possess
Him as thy slave, and now long-needy Fame
Doth e'en grow rich, naming my Stella's name,
Wit learns in thee perfection to express;
Not thou by praise, but praise in thee is rais'd:
It is a praise to praise when thou art prais'd.

Stella, *whence doth this new assault arise,*
A conquer'd, yielding, ransack'd heart to win,
Whereto long since, through my long-batter'd eyes,
Whole armies of thy beauties enter'd in?
And there, long since, Love thy lieutenant lies,
My fortress raz'd, thy banners rais'd within;
Of conquest do not these effects suffice,
But wilt now war upon thine own begin?
With so sweet voice, and by sweet Nature so
In sweetest strength, so sweetly skill'd withal,
In all sweet stratagems sweet Art can show,
That not my soul, which at thy foot did fall
Long since, forc'd by thy beams, but stone nor tree,
By Sense's privilege, can scape from thee!

My mouth doth water, and my breast doth swell,
My tongue doth itch, my thoughts in labour be;
Listen then, lordings, with good ear to me,
For of my life I must a riddle tell.
Towards Aurora's Court a nymph doth dwell,*
Rich in all beauties which man's eye can see;
Beauties so far from reach of words that we
Abase her praise saying she doth excel;
Rich in the treasure of deserv'd renown,
Rich in the riches of a royal heart,
Rich in those gifts which give th'eternal crown;
Who, though most rich in these and every part
Which make the patents of true worldly bliss,
Hath no misfortune but that Rich she is.

 38

This night, while sleep begins with heavy wings
To hatch* mine eyes, and that unbitted* thought
Doth fall to stray, and my chief powers are brought
To leave the sceptre of all subject things,
The first that straight my fancy's error brings
Unto my mind is Stella's image, wrought
By Love's own self, but with so curious draught
That she, methinks, not only shines but sings.
I start, look, hark; but what in clos'd-up sense
Was held, in open'd sense it flies away,
Leaving me nought but wailing eloquence.
I, seeing better sights in sight's decay,
Call'd it anew,* and wooèd Sleep again:
But him, her host, that unkind guest had slain.

39

Come, Sleep, O Sleep, the certain knot of peace,
The baiting-place of wit, the balm of woe,
The poor man's wealth, the prisoner's release,
The indifferent judge between the high and low!
With shield of proof shield me from out the prease*
Of those fierce darts Despair at me doth throw;
O make in me those civil wars to cease:
I will good tribute pay if thou do so.
Take thou of me smooth pillows, sweetest bed,
A chamber deaf to noise and blind to light,
A rosy garland and a weary head.
And if these things, as being thine by right,
Move not thy heavy grace, thou shalt in me,
Livelier than elsewhere, Stella's image see.

As good to write as for to lie and groan,
O Stella dear, how much thy power hath wrought,
That hast my mind—none of the basest—brought
My still-kept course, while others sleep, to moan!
Alas, if from the height of Virtue's throne
Thou canst vouchsafe the influence of a thought
Upon a wretch that long thy grace hath sought,
Weigh then how I by thee am overthrown;
And then think thus: although thy beauty be
Made manifest by such a victory,
Yet noblest conquerors do wrecks avoid.
Since then thou hast so far subduèd me,
That in my heart I offer still to thee,
O do not let thy temple be destroy'd!

41*

Having this day my horse, my hand, my lance
Guided so well that I obtain'd the prize,
Both by the judgment of the English eyes,
And of some sent from that sweet enemy France;
Horsemen my skill in horsemanship advance,
Townfolks my strength; a daintier judge applies
His praise to sleight which from good use doth rise;
Some lucky wits impute it but to chance;
Others, because of both sides I do take
*My blood from them who did excel in this,**
Think Nature me a man of arms did make.
How far they shoot awry! The true cause is,
Stella look'd on, and from her heavenly face
Sent forth the beams which made so fair my race.

42

O eyes which do the spheres of beauty move,
Whose beams be joys, whose joys all virtue be,
Who, while they make Love conquer, conquer Love;
The schools where Venus hath learn'd chastity.
O eyes, where humble looks most glorious prove,
Only-lov'd tyrants, just in cruelty,
Do not, O do not, from poor me remove;
Keep still my zenith,* ever shine on me.
For though I never see them but straightways
My life forgets to nourish languish'd sprites,
Yet still on me, O eyes, dart down your rays!
And if from majesty of sacred lights
Oppressing mortal sense my death proceed,
Wracks triumphs be which Love, high set, doth breed.

 *43*

Fair eyes, sweet lips, dear heart, that foolish I
Could hope by Cupid's help on you to prey,
Since to himself he doth your gifts apply
As his main force, choice sport and easeful stay;
For when he will see who dare him gainsay,
Then with those eyes he looks; lo, by and by
Each soul doth at Love's feet his weapons lay,
Glad if for her he give them leave to die.
When he will play, then in her lips he is,
Where, blushing red that Love's self them doth love,
With either lip he doth the other kiss;
But when he will for quiet's sake remove
From all the world, her heart is then his room,
Where well he knows no man to him can come.

My words I know do well set forth my mind;
My mind bemoans his sense of inward smart;
Such smart may pity claim of any heart;
Her heart, sweet heart, is of no tiger's kind—
And yet she hears, and yet no pity I find,
But more I cry, less grace she doth impart.
Alas, what cause is there so overthwart
That nobleness itself makes thus unkind?
I much do guess, yet find no truth save this,
That when the breath of my complaints doth touch
Those dainty doors unto the Court of Bliss,
The heavenly nature of that place is such
That, once come there, the sobs of mine annoys
Are metamorphos'd straight to tunes of joys.

 45

Stella *oft sees the very face of woe*
Painted in my beclouded stormy face,
But cannot skill* to pity my disgrace,
Not though thereof the cause herself she know;
Yet, hearing late a fable which did show
Of lovers never known a grievous case,
Pity thereof gat in her breast such place
That, from that sea deriv'd, tears' spring did flow.
Alas, if fancy, drawn by imag'd things
Though false, yet with free scope, more grace doth breed
Than servant's wrack, where new doubts honour brings!*
Then think, my dear, that you in me do read
Of lovers' ruin some sad tragedy;
I am not I: pity the tale of me.

I curs'd thee oft, I pity now thy case,
Blind-hitting Boy, since she that thee and me
Rules with a beck so tyranniseth thee
That thou must want or food or dwelling-place,
For she protests to banish thee her face.
Her face? O Love, a rogue thou then should'st be
If Love learn not alone to love and see
Without desire to feed of further grace!
Alas, poor wag, that now a scholar art
To such a schoolmistress, whose lessons new
Thou needs must miss, and so thou needs must smart.
Yet, dear, let me his pardon get of you,
So long—though he from book myche* to desire—
Till without fuel you can make hot fire.

What, have I thus betray'd my liberty?
Can those black beams such burning marks engrave
In my free side, or am I born a slave
Whose neck becomes such yoke of tyranny?
Or want I sense to feel my misery,
Or sprite disdain of such disdain to have,
Who for long faith, though daily help I crave,
May get no alms but scorn of beggary?
Virtue awake! Beauty but beauty is;
I may, I must, I can, I will, I do
Leave following that which it is gain to miss.
Let her go! Soft, but here she comes! 'Go to
Unkind, I love you not!' O me, that eye
Doth make my heart give to my tongue the lie!

Soul's joy, bend not those morning stars from me
Where Virtue is made strong by Beauty's might;
Where Love is chasteness, Pain doth learn delight,
And Humbleness grows one with Majesty.
Whatever may ensue, O let me be
Co-partner of the riches of that sight;
Let not mine eyes be hell-driv'n from that light,
O look, O shine, O let me die, and see!
For though I oft myself of them bemoan
That through my heart their beamy darts be gone
Whose cureless wounds e'en now most freshly bleed,
Yet since my death wound is already got,
Dear killer, spare not thy sweet cruel shot:
A kind of grace it is to slay with speed.

I on my horse, and Love on me, doth try
Our horsemanship, while by strange work I prove
A horseman to my horse, a horse to Love,
And now man's wrongs in me, poor beast, descry.
The reins wherewith my rider doth me tie
Are humbl'd thoughts, which bit of reverence move,
Curb'd in with fear, but with gilt boss above
Of hope, which makes it seem fair to the eye.
The wand is Will; thou, Fancy, saddle art,
Girt fast by Memory; and while I spur
My horse, he spurs with sharp desire my heart.
He sits me fast, however I do stir,
And now hath made me to his hand so right
That in the Manège* myself takes delight.

Stella, *the fullness of my thoughts of thee*
Cannot be stay'd within my panting breast,
But they do swell and struggle forth of me
Till that in words thy figure be express'd;
And yet as soon as they so formèd be,
According to my lord Love's own behest,
With sad eyes I their weak proportion see
To portrait that which in this world is best.
So that I cannot choose but write my mind,
And cannot choose but put out* what I write,
While these poor babes their death in birth do find.
And now my pen these lines had dashèd quite
But that they stopp'd his fury from the same,
Because their forefront bare sweet Stella's *name.*

Pardon mine ears, both I and they do pray,
So may your tongue still flauntingly proceed
To them that do such entertainment need,
So may you still have somewhat new to say.
On silly* me do not the burthen lay
Of all the grave conceits your brain doth breed,
But find some Hercules to bear, instead
Of Atlas tir'd, your wisdom's heavenly sway.
For me, while you discourse of courtly tides,
Of cunning fishers in most troublèd streams,
Of straying ways, when valiant Error guides,
Meanwhile my heart confers with Stella's *beams,*
And is e'en irk'd that so sweet comedy
By such unsuited speech should hinder'd be.

A strife is grown between Virtue and Love,
While each pretends that Stella must be his;
Her eyes, her lips, her all, saith Love, do this,
Since they do wear his badge, most firmly prove.
But Virtue thus that title doth disprove,
That Stella—O dear name!—that Stella is
That virtuous soul, sure heir of heavenly bliss,
Not this fair outside which our hearts doth move.
And therefore, though her beauty and her grace
Be Love's indeed, in Stella's self he may
By no pretence claim any manner place.
Well, Love, since this demur our suit doth stay,
Let Virtue have that Stella's self; yet thus—
That Virtue but that body grant to us.

53

In martial sports I had my cunning tried,
And yet to break more staves did me address,
While, with the people's shouts, I must confess
Youth, luck, and praise e'en fill'd my veins with
  pride.
When Cupid, having me his slave descried
In Mars's livery prancing in the press,
'What now, Sir Fool!' said he 'I would no less,
Look here, I say!' I look'd, and Stella spied,
Who hard by made a window send forth light.
My heart then quak'd, then dazzl'd were mine eyes,
One hand forgot to rule, th' other to fight,
Nor trumpet's sound I heard, nor friendly cries,
My foe came on, and beat the air for me,
Till that her blush taught me my shame to see.

Because I breathe not love to everyone,
Nor do not use set colours for to wear,
Nor nourish special locks of vowèd hair,
Nor give each speech a full point of a groan,
The courtly nymphs, acquainted with the moan
Of them who in their lips Love's standard bear,
'What, he?' say they of me, 'now I dare swear
He cannot love! No, no, let him alone!'
And think so still, so Stella know my mind.
Profess indeed I do not Cupid's art,
But you, fair maids, at length this true shall find,
That his right badge is but worn in the heart.
Dumb swans, not chatt'ring pies,* do lovers prove:
They love indeed who quake to say they love.

 55

Muses, I oft invok'd your holy aid,
With choicest flowers my speech to engarland so,
That it, despis'd, in true but naked show
Might win some grace in your sweet grace array'd;
And oft whole troups of saddest words I stay'd,
Striving abroad a-foraging to go,
Until by your inspiring I might know
How their black banner might be best display'd.
But now I mean no more your help to try,
Nor other sugaring of my speech to prove,
But on her name incessantly to cry;
For let me but name her whom I do love,
So sweet sounds straight mine ear and heart do hit,
That I well find no eloquence like it.

56

Fie, school of Patience, fie! Your lesson is
Far too long to learn it without book;
What, a whole week without one piece of look,
And think I should not your large precepts miss?
When I might read those letters fair of bliss
Which in her face teach virtue, I could brook
Somewhat thy leaden counsels, which I took
As of a friend that meant not much amiss.
But now that I, alas, do want her sight,
What, dost thou think that I can ever take
In thy cold stuff a phlegmatic delight?
No, Patience, if thou wilt my good, then make
Her come and hear with patience my desire,
And then with patience bid me bear my fire.

Woe having made with many fights his own
Each sense of mine, each gift, each power of mind
Grown now his slaves, he forc'd them out to find
The thoroughest words fit for Woe's self to groan,
Hoping that when they might find Stella alone,
Before she could prepare to be unkind,
Her soul, arm'd but with such a dainty rind,
Should soon be pierc'd with sharpness of the moan.
She heard my plaints, and did not only hear,
But them—so sweet is she—most sweetly sing,
With that fair breast making Woe's darkness clear.
A pretty case! I hopèd her to bring
To feel my griefs; and she with face and voice
So sweets my pains, that my pains me rejoice

Doubt there hath been when with his golden chain
The orator so far men's hearts doth bind
That no pace else their guided steps can find
But as he them more short or slack doth rein,
Whether with words the sovereignty he gain,
Cloth'd with fine tropes, with strongest reasons lin'd,★
Or else pronouncing grace, wherewith his mind
Prints his own lively form in rudest brain.
Now judge by this: in piercing phrases late
The anatomy of all my woes I wrate;★
Stella's *sweet breath the same to me did read.*
O voice! O face! Maugre★ *my speech's might,*
Which wooèd woe, most ravishing delight
E'en those sad words e'en in sad me did breed.

Dear, why make you more of a dog than me?
If he do love, I burn, I burn in love;
If he wait well, I never thence would move;
If he be fair, yet but a dog can be.
Little he is, so little worth is he;
He barks, my songs thine own voice oft doth prove;
Bidd'n, perhaps he fetcheth thee a glove,
But I, unbid, fetch e'en my soul to thee;
Yet while I languish, him that bosom clips,*
That lap doth lap, nay lets, in spite of spite,
This sour-breath'd mate taste of those sugar'd lips.
Alas, if you grant only such delight
To witless things, then Love, I hope—since wit
Becomes a clog—will soon ease me of it.

 60

When my good angel guides me to the place
Where all my good I do in Stella see,
That heaven of joys throws only down on me
Thunder'd disdains and lightnings of disgrace;
But when the rugged'st step of Fortune's race
Makes me fall from her sight, then sweetly she,
With words wherein the Muses' treasures be,
Shows love and pity to my absent case.
Now I, wit-beaten long by hardest Fate,
So dull am that I cannot look into
The ground of this fierce love and lovely hate.
Then, some good body, tell me how I do,
Whose presence absence, absence presence is,
Bless'd in my curse, and cursèd in my bliss.

61

Oft with true sighs, oft with uncallèd tears,
Now with slow words, now with dumb eloquence,
I Stella's eyes assail, invade her ears,
But this at last is her sweet-breath'd defence:
'That who indeed infelt affection bears
So captives to his saint both soul and sense
That, wholly hers, all selfness he forbears,
Thence his desires he learns, his life's course thence.'
Now since her chaste mind I straight must show that she
Shall quickly me from what she hates remove.
O Doctor Cupid, thou for me reply,
Driven else to grant, by angel's sophistry,
That I love not without I leave to love.

62

Late tir'd with woe, e'en ready for to pine
With rage of Love, I call'd my Love unkind;
She in whose eyes love, though unfelt, doth shine,
Sweet said that I true love in her should find.
I joy'd, but straight thus water'd was my wine:
That love she did, but lov'd a love not blind,
Which would not let me whom she lov'd decline
From noble course fit for my birth and mind.
And therefore, by her love's authority,
Will'd me these tempests of vain love to fly,
And anchor fast myself on Virtue's shore.
Alas, if this the only metal be
Of love new-coin'd to help my beggary,
Dear, love me not, that you may love me more.

O grammar rules, O now your virtues show,
So children still read you with awful eyes,
As my young dove may in your precepts wise
Her grant to me by her own virtue know.
For late, with heart most high, with eyes most low,
I crav'd the thing which ever she denies;
She, lightning love, displaying Venus' skies,
Lest once should not be heard, twice said: 'No, no!'
Sing then, my Muse, now 'Io Pæan' sing;
Heavens envy not at my high triumphing,
But grammar's force with sweet success confirm:
For grammar says—O this, dear Stella, say!—
For grammar says—to grammar who says nay?—
That in one speech two negatives affirm!

FIRST SONG

Doubt you to whom my Muse these notes intendeth,
Which now my breast, o'ercharg'd, to music lendeth?
To you, to you, all song of praise is due:
Only in you my song begins and endeth.

Who hath the eyes which marry state with pleasure?
Who keeps the key of Nature's chiefest treasure?
To you, to you, all song of praise is due:
Only for you the heaven forgot all measure.

Who hath the lips where wit in fairness reigneth?
Who womankind at once both decks and staineth?*
To you, to you, all song of praise is due:
Only by you Cupid his crown maintaineth.

Who hath the feet whose step all sweetness planteth?
Who else, for whom Fame worthy trumpets wanteth?
To you, to you, all song of praise is due:
Only to you her sceptre Venus granteth.

Who hath the breast whose milk doth passions nourish?
Whose grace is such that when it chides doth cherish?

To you, to you, all song of praise is due:
Only through you the tree of life doth flourish.

Who hath the hand which without stroke subdueth?
Who long dead beauty with increase reneweth?
To you, to you, all song of praise is due:
Only at you all envy hopeless rueth.

Who hath the hair which, loosest, fasteth tieth?
Who makes a man live, then glad when he dieth?
To you, to you, all song of praise is due:
Only of you the flatterer never lieth.

Who hath the voice which soul from senses sunders?
Whose force but yours the bolts of beauty thunders?
To you, to you, all song of praise is due:
Only with you not miracles are wonders.

Doubt you to whom my Muse these notes intendeth,
Which now my breast, o'ercharg'd, to music lendeth?
To you, to you, all song of praise is due:
Only in you my song begins and endeth.

No more, my dear, no more these counsels try;
O give my passions leave to run their race;
Let fortune lay on me her worst disgrace;
Let folk o'ercharg'd with brain against me cry;
Let clouds bedim my face, break in mine eye;
Let me no steps but of lost labour trace;
Let all the earth with scorn recount my case—
But do not will me from my love to fly.
I do not envy Aristotle's wit,
Nor do aspire to Caesar's bleeding fame,
Nor aught do care though some above me sit,
Nor hope, nor wish another course to frame,
But that which once may win thy cruel heart:
Thou art my wit, and thou my virtue art.

 65

Love, by sure proof I may call thee unkind
That giv'st no better ear to my just cries,
Thou whom to me such my good turns should bind
As I may well recount, but none can prize:*
For when, naked Boy, thou could'st no harbour find
In this old world grown now so too too wise,
I lodg'd thee in my heart, and being blind
By nature born, I gave to thee mine eyes.
Mine eyes, my light, my heart, my life, alas!
If so great services may scornèd be,
Yet let this thought thy tigerish courage pass,
That I perhaps am somewhat kin to thee,
Since in thine arms, if learn'd fame truth hath spread,
Thou bear'st the arrow, I the arrow-head.*

66

And do I see some cause a hope to feed,
Or doth the tedious burden of long woe
In weaken'd minds quick apprehending breed
Of every image which may comfort show?
I cannot brag of word, much less of deed;
Fortune wheels still with me in one sort slow;
My wealth no more, and no whit less my need;
Desire still on stilts* of fear doth go.
And yet amid all fears a hope there is,
Stol'n to my heart since last fair night, nay day,
Stella's *eyes sent to me the beams of bliss,*
Looking on me while I look'd other way;
But when mine eyes back to their heaven did move,
They fled with blush which guilty seem'd of love.

Hope, art thou true, or dost thou flatter me?
Doth Stella *now* begin with piteous eye
The ruins of her conquest to espy?
Will she take time* before all wrackèd* be?
Her eyes-speech is translated thus by thee,
But fail'st thou not in phrase so heavenly high?
Look on't again, the fair text better try,
What blushing notes dost thou in margin see?
What sighs stol'n out, or kill'd before full-born?
Hast thou found such and such-like arguments?
Or art thou else to comfort me forsworn?
Well, howso thou interpret the contents,
I am resolv'd thy error to maintain,
Rather than by more truth to get more pain.

 68

Stella, *the only planet of my night,*
Light of my life, and life of my desire,
Chief good whereto my hope doth only aspire,
World of my wealth, and heaven of my delight,
Why dost thou spend the treasures of thy sprite
With voice more fit to wed Amphion's lyre,
Seeking to quench in me the noble fire
Fed by thy worth, and kindled by thy sight?
And all in vain: for while thy breath most sweet
With choicest words, thy words with reasons rare,
Thy reasons firmly set on Virtue's feet,
Labour to kill in me this killing care,
O think I then what paradise of joy
It is, so fair a virtue to enjoy!

 69

O joy, too high for my low style to show!
O bliss, fit for a nobler state than me!
Envy, put out thine eyes, lest thou do see
What oceans of delight in me do flow!
My friend, that oft saw through all masks my woe,
Come, come, and let me pour myself on thee;
Gone is the Winter of my misery:
My Spring appears—O see what here doth grow!
For Stella hath, with words where faith doth shine,
Of her high heart given me the monarchy.
I, I, oh I, may say that she is mine,
And though she give but thus conditionly
This realm of bliss, while virtuous course I take,
No kings be crown'd but they some covenants make.

My Muse may well grudge at my heavenly joy,
If still I force her in sad rhymes to creep;
She oft hath drunk my tears, now hopes to enjoy
Nectar of mirth, since I Jove's cup do keep.
Sonnets be not bound prentice to annoy;
Trebles sing high, as well as basses deep;
Grief but Love's winter livery is; the Boy
Hath cheeks to smile, as well as eyes to weep.
Come then, my Muse, show thou height of delight
In well-rais'd notes; my pen, the best it may,
Shall paint our joy, though but in black and white.
Cease, eager Muse; peace, pen, for my sake stay;
I give you here my hand for truth of this—
Wise silence is best music unto bliss.

Who will in fairest book of Nature know
How virtue may best lodg'd in beauty be,
Let him but learn of Love to read in thee,
Stella, those fair lines which true goodness show.
There shall he find all vice's overthrow,
Not by rude force, but sweetest sovreignty
Of reason, from whose light those night-birds fly,
That inward sun in thine eyes shineth so.
And not content to be Perfection's heir
Thyself, dost strive all minds that way to move
Who mark in thee what is in thee most fair.
So while thy beauty draws the heart to love,
As fast thy virtue bends that love to good.
But ah, Desire still cries: 'Give me some food!'

Desire, though thou my old companion art,
And oft so clings to my pure love that I
One from the other scarcely can descry,
While each doth blow the fire of my heart,
Now from thy fellowship I needs must part:
Venus is taught with Dian's wings to fly;
I must no more in thy sweet passions lie:
Virtue's gold now must head my Cupid's dart.
Service and honour, wonder with delight,
Fear to offend, will worthy to appear,
Care shining in mine eyes, faith in my sprite,
These things are left me by my only Dear;
But thou, Desire, because thou would'st have all,
Now banish'd art—but yet, alas, how shall?

SECOND SONG

Have I caught my heavenly jewel
Teaching Sleep most fair to be?
Now will I teach her that she,
When she wakes, is too too cruel.

Since sweet Sleep her eyes hath charmèd,
The two only darts of Love,
Now will I with that Boy prove
Some play while he is disarmèd.

Her tongue, waking, still refuseth,
Giving frankly niggard 'No';
Now will I attempt to know
What 'No' her tongue, sleeping, useth.

See the hand which, waking, guardeth,
Sleeping, grants a free resort;
Now will I invade the fort—
Cowards Love with loss rewardeth.

But, O fool, think of the danger
Of her just and high disdain!

Now will I, alas, refrain;
Love fears nothing else but anger.

Yet those lips, so sweetly swelling,
Do invite a stealing kiss;
Now will I but venture this:
Who will read must first learn spelling.

O, sweet kiss! but ah, she's waking!
Lowring beauty chastens me;
Now will I away hence flee:
Fool, more fool, for no more taking!

73

Love still a boy and oft a wanton is,
School'd only by his mother's tender eye;
What wonder then if he his lesson miss,
When for so soft a rod dear play he try?
And yet my Star, because a sugar'd kiss
In sport I suck'd while she asleep did lie,
Doth lower, nay chide, nay threat for only this;
Sweet, it was saucy Love, not humble I.
But no 'scuse serves; she makes her wrath appear
In Beauty's throne. See now, who dares come near
Those scarlet judges threatening bloody pain?
O heavenly fool, thy most kiss-worthy face
Anger invests with such a lovely grace
That Anger's self I needs must kiss again.

I never drank of Aganippe well,*
Nor ever did in shade of Tempe* sit,
And Muses scorn with vulgar brains to dwell;
Poor layman, I, for sacred rites unfit.
Some do I hear of poets' fury tell,
But, God wot, wot not what they mean by it;
And this I swear by blackest brook of hell,
I am no pick-purse of another's wit.
How falls it then that with so smooth an ease
My thoughts I speak, and what I speak doth flow
In verse, and that my verse best wits doth please?
Guess we the cause? What, is it thus? Fie, no.
Or so? Much less. How then? Sure thus it is:
My lips are sweet, inspired with Stella's kiss.

75*

Of all the kings that ever here did reign,
Edward, nam'd fourth, as first in praise I name:
Not for his fair outside nor well-lin'd brain,
Although less gifts imp feathers* oft on fame:
Nor that he could, young-wise, wise-valiant, frame
His sire's revenge, join'd with a kingdom's gain,
And gain'd by Mars, could yet mad Mars so tame
That balance weigh'd what sword did late obtain:
Nor that he made the flower-de-luce so 'fraid,
Though strongly hedg'd, of bloody lions' paws,
That witty Lewis to him a tribute paid.
Nor this, nor that, nor any such small cause,
But only for this worthy knight durst prove
To lose his crown rather than fail his love.

76

She comes, and straight therewith her shining twins do
   move
Their rays to me who in their tedious absence lay
Benighted in cold woe; but now appears my day,
The only light of joy, the only warmth of love.
She comes with light and warmth which, like Aurora,
   prove
Of gentle force, so that mine eyes dare gladly play
With such a rosy morn whose beams, most freshly gay,
Scorch not, but only do dark chilling sprites remove.
But, lo, while I do speak, it groweth noon with me,
Her flamy-glistring lights increase with time and place,
My heart cries, 'O it burns!' mine eyes now dazzl'd be;
No wind, no shade can cool: what help then in my case?
But with short breath, long looks, stay'd feet and
   walking head,*
Pray that my sun go down with meeker beams to bed.

Those looks, whose beams be joy, whose motion is delight,
That face whose lecture shows what perfect beauty is,
That presence which doth give dark hearts a living light,
That grace which Venus weeps that she herself doth
    miss,
That hand which without touch holds more than Atlas
    might,
Those lips which make death's pay a mean price for a
    kiss,
That skin whose past-praise hue scorns this poor term
    of white,
Those words which do sublime the quintessence of bliss,
That voice which makes the soul plant himself in the ears,
That conversation sweet where such high comforts be
As, conster'd*in true speech, the name of heaven it bears:
Makes me in my best thoughts and quietest judgment see
That in no more but these I might be fully bless'd.
Yet, ah, my maiden Muse doth blush to tell the best.

O how the pleasant airs of true love be
Infected by those vapours which arise
From out that noisome gulf which gaping lies
Between the jaws of hellish Jealousy!
A monster, others' harm, self-misery,
Beauty's plague, Virtue's scourge, succour of lies,
Who his own joy to his own hurt applies,
And only cherish doth with injury;
Who since he hath by Nature's special grace
So piercing paws as spoil when they embrace,
So nimble feet as stir still, though on thorns,
So many eyes aye seeking their own woe,
So ample ears as never good news know:
Is it not evil that such a devil wants horns?

Sweet kiss, thy sweets I fain would sweetly indite
Which even of sweetness sweetest sweetener art,
Pleasing'st consort,* where each sense holds a part,
Which, coupling doves, guides Venus' chariot right;
Best charge and bravest retreat in Cupid's fight,
A double key which opens to the heart,
Most rich when most his riches it impart;
Nest of young joys, schoolmaster of delight,
Teaching the mean at once to take and give;
The friendly fray, where blows both wound and heal,
The pretty death, while each in other live;
Poor hope's first wealth, hostage of promis'd weal,
Breakfast of love. But lo, lo, where she is,
Cease we to praise: now pray we for a kiss.

 *80*

Sweet-swelling lip, well may'st thou swell in pride,
Since best wits think it wit thee to admire;
Nature's praise, Virtue's stall;* Cupid's cold fire,
Whence words, not words but heavenly graces slide;
The new Parnassus, where the Muses bide,
Sweetner of music, Wisdom's beautifier,
Breather of life, and fastner of desire,
Where Beauty's blush in Honour's grain is dyed.
Thus much my heart compell'd my mouth to say;
But now, spite of my heart, my mouth will stay,
Loathing all lies, doubting this flattery is:
And no spur can his resty* race renew
Without—how far this praise is short of you—
Sweet lip, you teach my mouth with one sweet kiss.

 *81*

O kiss, which dost those ruddy gems impart,
Or gems or fruits of new-found Paradise,
Breathing all bliss and sweetning to the heart,
Teaching dumb lips a nobler exercise;
O kiss, which souls, e'en souls, together ties
By links of love and only Nature's art,
How fain would I paint thee to all men's eyes,
Or of thy gifts at least shade out* some part!
But she forbids; with blushing words she says
She builds her fame on higher-seated praise.
But my heart burns; I cannot silent be.
Then since, dear life, you fain would have me peace,
And I, mad with delight, want wit to cease,
Stop you my mouth with still, still kissing me.

Nymph of the garden where all beauties be,
Beauties which do in excellency pass
His who till death look'd in a watery glass,
Or hers whom naked the Trojan boy did see;
Sweet garden-nymph, which keeps the cherry-tree
Whose fruit doth far the Hesperian taste surpass,
Most sweet-fair, most fair-sweet, do not, alas,
From coming near those cherries banish me.
For though, full of desire, empty of wit,
Admitted late by your best-gracèd grace,
I caught at one of them a hungry bit,
Pardon that fault; once more grant me the place,
And I do swear, e'en by the same delight,
I will but kiss, I never more will bite.

Good brother Philip,* I have borne you long;
I was content you should in favour creep,
While craftily you seem'd your cut to keep,*
As though that fair soft hand did you great wrong.
I bare with envy, yet I bare your song,
When in her neck you did love-ditties peep;
Nay—more fool I—oft suffer'd you to sleep
In lilies' nest where Love's self lies along.
What, doth high place ambitious thoughts augment?
Is sauciness reward of courtesy?
Cannot such grace your silly self content
But you must needs with those lips billing be,
And through those lips drink nectar from that tongue?
Leave that, Sir Phip, lest off your neck be wrung!

THIRD SONG

If Orpheus' voice had force to breathe such music's love
Through pores of senseless trees as it could make them move,
If stones good measure danc'd the Theban walls to build
To cadence of the tunes which Amphion's lyre did yield,
More cause a like effect at leastwise bringeth:
O stones, O trees, learn hearing—Stella singeth!

If love might sweeten so a boy of shepherd brood
To make a lizard dull to taste love's dainty food,
If eagle fierce could so in Grecian maid delight,
As his light was her eyes, her death his endless night—
Earth gave that love, heaven I trow love refineth—
O birds, O beasts, look, love: lo, Stella shineth!

The birds, beasts, stones, and trees feel this, and feeling,
    love;
And if the trees nor stones stir not the same to prove,
Nor beasts nor birds do come unto this blessèd gaze,
Know that small love is quick, and great love doth amaze.
They are amaz'd, but you, with reason armèd,
O eyes, O ears of men, how are you charmèd!

Highway, since you my chief Parnassus be,
And that my Muse, to some ears not unsweet,
Tempers her words to trampling horses' feet
More oft than to a chamber melody,
Now blessèd you, bear onward blessèd me
To her where I my heart, safe-left, shall meet:
My Muse and I must you of duty greet
With thanks and wishes, wishing thankfully.
Be you still careful kept by public heed,
By no encroachment wrong'd, nor time forgot,
Nor blam'd for blood, nor sham'd for sinful deed,
And, that you know I envy you no lot
Of highest wish, I wish you so much bliss,
Hundreds of years you Stella's feet may kiss!

 85

I see the house: my heart thyself contain!
Beware full sails drown not thy tottering barge,
Lest joy, by nature apt sprites to enlarge,
Thee to thy wrack beyond thy limits strain;
Nor do like lords whose weak confusèd brain,
Not 'pointing to fit folks each undercharge,
While every office themselves will discharge,
With doing all leave nothing done but pain;
But give apt servants their due place: let eyes
See beauty's total sum summ'd in her face,
Let ears hear speech which wit to wonder ties,
Let breath suck up those sweets, let arms embrace
The globe of weal,★ lips Love's indentures make:
Thou but of all the kingly tribute take.

FOURTH SONG

Only joy, now here you are,
Fit to hear and ease my care;
Let my whispering voice obtain
Sweet reward for sharpest pain:
Take me to thee, and thee to me.
'No, no, no, no, my dear, let be.'

Night hath clos'd all in her cloak,
Twinkling stars love-thoughts provoke,
Danger hence good care doth keep,
Jealousy himself doth sleep;
Take me to thee, and thee to me.
'No, no, no, no, my dear, let be.'

Better place no wit can find,
Cupid's yoke to loose or bind;
These sweet flowers, on fine bed too,
Us in their best language woo:
Take me to thee, and thee to me.
'No, no, no, no, my dear, let be.'

This small light the moon bestows,
Serves thy beams but to disclose,

So to raise my hap more high;
Fear not else, none can us spy.
Take me to thee, and thee to me.
'No, no, no, no, my dear, let be.'

That you heard was but a mouse,
Dumb sleep holdeth all the house;
Yet asleep, methinks, they say:
'Young fools, take time while you may.'
Take me to thee, and thee to me.
'No, no, no, no, my dear, let be.'

Niggard Time threats, if we miss
This large offer of our bliss,
Long stay ere he grant the same;
Sweet, then, while each thing doth frame,
Take me to thee, and thee to me.
'No, no, no, no, my dear, let be.'

Your fair mother is abed,
Candles out and curtains spread;
She thinks you do letters write;
Write, but let me first indite:
Take me to thee, and thee to me.
'No, no, no, no, my dear, let be.'

Sweet, alas, why strive you thus?
Concord better fitteth us.
Leave to Mars the force of hands;
Your power in your beauty stands.
Take me to thee, and thee to me.
'No, no, no, no, my dear, let be.'

Woe to me, and do you swear
Me to hate but I forbear?
Cursèd be my destines all
That brought me so high to fall.
Soon with my death I will please thee.
'No, no, no, no, my dear, let be.'

Alas, whence came this change of looks? If I
Have chang'd desert let mine own conscience be
A still-felt plague to self-condemning me,
Let woe gripe on my heart, shame load mine eye.
But if all faith like spotless ermine lie
Safe in my soul, which only doth to thee
As his sole object of felicity
With wings of love in air of wonder fly,
O ease your hand, treat not so hard your slave:
In justice pains come not till faults do call.
Or if I needs, sweet judge, must torments have,
Use something else to chasten me withal
Than those bless'd eyes where all my hopes do dwell:
No doom should make one's heaven become his hell.

FIFTH SONG

While favour fed my hope, delight with hope was brought,
Thought waited on delight and speech did follow thought;
Then grew my tongue and pen records unto thy glory.
I thought all words were lost that were not spent of thee;
I thought each place was dark but where thy lights would
   be,
And all ears worse than deaf that heard not out thy story.

I said thou wert most fair, and so indeed thou art;
I said thou wert most sweet sweet poison to my heart;
I said my soul was thine—O that I then had lied—
I said thine eyes were stars, thy breasts the milken way,
Thy fingers Cupid's shafts, thy voice the angels' lay;
And all I said so well, as no man it denied.

But now that hope is lost, unkindness kills delight;
Yet thought and speech do live, though metamorphos'd quite,
For rage now rules the reins which guided were by pleasure.
I think now of thy faults, who late thought of thy praise,
That speech falls now to blame, which did thy honour raise:
The same key open can which can lock up a treasure.

Thou then whom partial heavens conspir'd in one to frame
The proof of Beauty's worth, the inheritrix of fame,
The mansion seat of bliss, and just excuse of lovers,
See now those feathers pluck'd wherewith thou flew most
    high,
See what clouds of reproach shall dark thy honour's sky:
Whose own fault casts him down, hardly high seat re-
    covers.

And O my Muse—though oft you lull'd her in your lap,
And then a heavenly child gave her ambrosian pap,
And to that brain of hers your hiddenest gifts infus'd—
Since she, disdaining me, doth you in me disdain,
Suffer not her to laugh while both we suffer pain:
Princes, in subjects wrong'd, must deem themselves abus'd.

Your client, poor myself, shall Stella handle so?
Revenge, revenge, my Muse! Defiance trumpet blow!
Threaten what may be done, yet do more than you threaten.
Ah, my suit granted is, I feel my breast to swell!
Now, child, a lesson new you shall begin to spell:
Sweet babes must babies* have, but shrewd girls must be
    beaten!

112

Think now no more to hear of warm, fine-odour'd snow,
Nor blushing lilies, nor pearls' ruby-hidden row,
Nor of that golden sea whose waves in curls are broken,
But of thy soul, so fraught with ungratefulness,
As where thou soon might'st help, most there thou dost
    oppress:
Ungrateful who is call'd, the worst of evils is spoken.

Yet worse than worst, I say thou art a thief. A thief?
Now God forbid! A thief, and of worst thieves the chief!
Thieves steal for need, and steal but goods which pain
    recovers,
But thou, rich in all joys, dost rob my joys from me,
Which cannot be restor'd by time nor industry:
Of foes the spoil is evil; far worse of constant lovers.

Yet gentle English thieves do rob but will not slay;
Thou, English murdering thief, wilt have hearts for thy
    prey!
The name of murderer now on thy fair forehead sitteth,
And e'en while I do speak my death wounds bleeding be,
Which I protest proceed from only cruel thee:
Who may and will not save, murder in truth committeth.

But murder private fault seems but a toy to thee;
I lay, then, to thy charge unjustest tyranny!
If rule by force without all claim a tyrant showeth—
For thou dost lord my heart who am not born thy slave,
And, which is worse, makes me most guiltless torments
  have—
A rightful prince by unright deeds a tyrant groweth.

Lo! you grow proud with this, for tyrants make folk bow;
Of foul rebellion, then, I do appeach* thee now!
Rebel by Nature's law, rebel by law of reason,
Thou sweetest subject wert born in the realm of Love,
And yet against thy Prince thy force dost daily prove:
No virtue merits praise once touch'd with blot of treason.

But valiant rebels oft in fools' mouths purchase fame,
I now then stain thy white with blackest blot of shame!
Both rebel to the son and vagrant from the mother;
For, wearing Venus' badge in every part of thee,
Unto Diana's train thou, runaway, did'st flee:
Who faileth one is false, though trusty to another.

114

What, is not this enough? Nay, far worse cometh here:
A witch I say thou art, though thou so fair appear!
For I protest my sight never thy face enjoyeth
But I in me am chang'd; I am alive and dead,
My feet are turn'd to roots, my heart becometh lead:
No witchcraft is so evil as which man's mind destroyeth.

Yet witches may repent; thou art far worse than they;
Alas that I am forc'd such evil of thee to say!
I say thou art a devil, though cloth'd in angels' shining,
For thy face tempts my soul to leave the heaven for thee,
And thy words of refuse do pour e'en hell on me:
Who tempt, and tempted plague, are devils in true defining.

You then ungrateful thief! You murdering tyrant, you!
You rebel runaway,★ to Lord and Lady untrue!
You witch! You devil! Alas, you still of me belovèd!
You see what I can say! Mend yet your froward mind,
And such skill in my Muse you reconcil'd shall find
That all these cruel words your praises shall be provèd.

SIXTH SONG

O you that hear this voice,
O you that see this face,
Say whether* of the choice
Deserves the former place:
Fear not to judge this bate,*
For it is void of hate.

This side doth Beauty take,
For that doth Music speak,
Fit orators to make
The strongest judgments weak:
The bar to plead their right
Is only true delight.

Thus doth the voice and face,
These gentle lawyers wage,
Like loving brothers' case,
For father's heritage;
That each, while each contends,
Itself to other lends.

For Beauty beautifies
With heavenly hue and grace

The heavenly harmonies,
And in this faultless face
The perfect beauties be
A perfect harmony.

Music more loftily swells
In speeches nobly plac'd,
Beauty as far excels
In action aptly grac'd.
A friend each party draws
To countenance his cause.

Love more affected seems
To Beauty's lovely light,
And Wonder more esteems
Of Music's wondrous might;
But both to both so bent,
As both in both are spent.

Music doth witness call
The ear his truth to try,
Beauty brings to the hall
The judgment of the eye:
Both in their objects such
As no exceptions touch.*

The common sense,* which might
Be arbiter of this,
To be forsooth upright,
To both sides partial is:
He lays on his chief praise,
Chief praise on that he lays.

Then Reason, princess high,
Whose throne is in the mind,
Which Music can in sky
And hidden beauties find,
Say whether thou wilt crown
With limitless renown?

SEVENTH SONG

Whose senses in so evil consort their stepdame, Nature, lays,
That ravishing delight in them most sweet tunes do not raise;*
Or if they do delight therein, yet are so closed with wit
As with sententious lips to to set a title vain on it:
O let them hear these sacred tunes, and learn in Wonder's
  schools
To be, in things past bounds of wit, fools, if they be not fools.

Who have so leaden eyes as not to see sweet Beauty's show,
Or, seeing, have so wooden wits as not that worth to know;
Or, knowing, have so muddy minds as not to be in love;
Or, loving, have so frothy thoughts as easily thence to move:
O let them see these heavenly beams, and in fair letters read
A lesson fit both sight and skill, love and firm love, to breed.

Hear then, but then with wonder hear; see, but adoring see;
No mortal gifts, no earthly fruits, now here descended be!
See—do you see this face? A face? Nay image of the skies,
Of which the two life-giving lights are figured in her eyes!
Hear you this soul-invading voice and count it but a voice?
The very essence of their tunes when angels do rejoice!

EIGHTH SONG

In a grove most rich of shade,
Where birds wanton music made,
May, then young, his pied weeds showing,
New-perfum'd with flowers fresh growing.

Astrophel *with* Stella *sweet*
Did for mutual comfort meet,
Both within themselves oppressèd,
But each in the other blessèd.

Him great harms had taught much care:
Her fair neck a foul yoke bare:
But her sight his cares did banish;
In his sight her yoke did vanish.

Wept they had, alas the while!
But now tears themselves did smile,
While their eyes, by love directed,
Interchangeably reflected.

Sigh they did, but now betwixt
Sighs of woe were glad sighs mix'd,
With arms crossed yet testifying
Restless rest and living dying.

Their ears hungry of each word
Which the dear tongue would afford,
But their tongues restrain'd from walking
Till their hearts had ended talking.

But, when their tongues could not speak,
Love itself did silence break;
Love did set his lips asunder,
Thus to speak in love and wonder:

'Stella, sovereign of my joy,
Fair triumpher of annoy,
Stella, star of heavenly fire,
Stella, lodestar of desire,

'Stella, in whose shining eyes
Are the lights of Cupid's skies,
Whose beams, where they once are darted,
Love therewith is straight imparted,

'Stella whose voice, when it speaks,
Senses all asunder breaks,
Stella whose voice, when it singeth,
Angels to acquaintance bringeth,

'Stella, *in whose body is*
Writ each character of bliss,
Whose face all, all beauty passeth,
Save thy mind, which yet surpasseth:

'Grant, O grant—but speech, alas,
Fails me, fearing on to pass!—
Grant, O me! what am I saying?
But no fault there is in praying.

'Grant, O dear, on knees I pray,'
(Knees on ground he then did stay)
'That, not I, but, since I love you,
Time and place for me may move you.

'Never season was more fit,
Never room more apt for it;
Smiling air allows my reason;
These birds sing, "Now use the season."

'This small wind, which so sweet is,
See how it the leaves doth kiss;
Each tree in his best attiring,
Sense of love to love inspiring.

'Love makes earth the water drink,
Love to earth makes water sink;
And, if dumb things be so witty,
Shall a heavenly grace want pity?'

There his hands, in their speech, fain
Would have made tongue's language plain;
But her hands, his hands repelling,
Gave repulse all grace excelling.

Then she spake; her speech was such,
As not ears but heart did touch:
While suchwise she love denièd,
As yet love she signifièd.

'Astrophel,' said she, 'my love
Cease in these effects* to prove;
Now be still, yet still believe me,
Thy grief more than death would grieve me.

'If that any thought in me
Can taste comfort but of thee,
Let me, fed with hellish anguish,
Joyless, hopeless, endless languish.

'If those eyes you praisèd be
Half so dear as you to me,
Let me home return, stark blinded
Of those eyes, and blinder minded.

'If to secret of my heart
I do any wish impart
Where thou are not foremost placèd,
Be both wish and I defacèd.

'If more may be said, I say
All my bliss in thee I lay;
If thou love, my love, content thee,
For all love, all faith, is meant thee.

'Trust me while I thee deny,
In myself the smart I try;
Tyrant honour doth thus use thee:
Stella's self might not refuse thee.

'Therefore, dear, this no more move,
Lest, though I leave not thy love,
Which too deep in me is framèd,
I should blush when thou art namèd.'

Therewithal away she went,
Leaving him so passion-rent
With what she had done and spoken,
That therewith my song is broken.

NINTH SONG

Go, my flock, go get you hence,
Seek a better place of feeding,
Where you may have some defence
From the storms in my heart breeding,
And showers from mine eyes proceeding.

Leave a wretch in whom all woe
Can abide to keep no measure;
Merry flock, such one forgo,
Unto whom mirth is displeasure,
Only rich in mischief's treasure.

Yet, alas, before you go,
Hear your woeful master's story,
Which to stones I else would show:
Sorrow only then hath glory
When 'tis excellently sorry.

Stella, fiercest shepherdess,
Fiercest but yet fairest ever,
Stella whom, O heavens, still bless,
Though against me she persever,
Though I bliss inherit never,

Stella *hath refusèd me,*
Stella *who more love hath provèd*
In this caitiff heart to be
Than can in good ewes be movèd
Toward lambkins best belovèd.

Stella *hath refusèd me,*
Astrophel, *that so well servèd,*
In this pleasant spring must see,
While in pride flowers be preservèd,
Himself only winter-starvèd.

Why, alas, doth she then swear
That she loveth me so dearly,
Seeing me so long to bear
Coals of love that burn so clearly,
And yet leave me helpless merely?

Is that love? Forsooth I trow,
If I saw my good dog grievèd,
And a help for him did know,
My love should not be believèd
But he were by me relievèd.

No, she hates me—wellaway!—
Feigning love somewhat to please me,
For she knows if she display
All her hate death soon would seize me
And of hideous torments ease me.

Then adieu, dear flock, adieu!
But, alas, if in your straying
Heavenly Stella *meet with you,*
*Tell her, in your piteous blaying,**
Her poor slave's unjust decaying.

When I was forc'd from Stella ever dear—
Stella, food of my thoughts, heart of my heart,
Stella, whose eyes make all my tempests clear—
By iron laws of duty to depart,
Alas, I found that she with me did smart:
I saw that tears did in her eyes appear,
I saw that sighs her sweetest lips did part,
And her sad words my sadded sense did hear.
For me, I wept to see pearls scatt'rèd so,
I sigh'd her sighs and wailèd for her woe,
Yet swam in joy, such love in her was seen.
Thus, while the effect most bitter was to me,
And nothing than the cause more sweet could be,
I had been vex'd, if vex'd I had not been.

88

Out, traitor *Absence*, darest thou counsel me
From my dear captainess to run away
Because in brave array here marcheth she
That to win me oft shows a present pay?
Is faith so weak? Or is such force in thee?
When sun is hid, can stars such beams display?
Cannot heaven's food, once felt, keep stomachs free
From base desire on earthly cates* to prey?
Tush, *Absence!* While thy mists eclipse that light,
My orphan sense flies to the inward sight,
Where memory sets forth the beams of love,
That, where before heart lov'd and eyes did see,
In heart both sight and love now couplèd be:
United powers make each the stronger prove.

 89

Now that of absence the most irksome night
With darkest shade doth overcome my day,
Since Stella's eyes, wont to give me my day,
Leaving my hemisphere leave me in night,
Each day seems long and longs for long-stay'd night;
The night, as tedious, woos the approach of day;
Tir'd with the dusty toils of busy day,
Languish'd with horrors of the silent night;
Suffering the evils both of day and night,
While no night is more dark than is my day,
Nor no day hath less quiet than my night:
With such bad mixture of my night and day,
That living thus in blackest winter night,
I feel the flames of hottest summer day.

90

Stella, *think not that I by verse seek fame*
Who seek, who hope, who love, who live but thee;
Thine eyes my pride, thy lips mine history:
If thou praise not, all other praise is shame.
Nor so ambitious am I as to frame
A nest for my young praise in laurel tree:
In truth I swear, I wish not there should be
Grav'd in my epitaph a poet's name.
Nay, if I would, could I just title make,
That any laud* thereof to me should grow,
Without my plumes from others' wings I take:
For nothing from my wit or will doth flow,
Since all my words thy beauty doth indite,
And Love doth hold my hand and makes me write.

 *91*

Stella, *while now by Honour's cruel might*
I am from you, light of my life, misled,
And that fair you, my sun, thus overspread
With Absence' veil, I live in Sorrow's night,
If this dark place yet show like candlelight
Some beauty's piece, as amber-colour'd head,
Milk hands, rose cheeks, or lips more sweet, more red;
Or seeing jets black* but in blackness bright;
They please, I do confess they please mine eyes;
But why? Because of you they models be,
Models such be wood-globes of glist'ring skies.
Dear, therefore be not jealous over me,
If you hear that they seem my heart to move:
Not them, O no, but you in them I love.

Be your words made, good Sir, of Indian ware,
That you allow me then by so small rate?
Or do you cutted* Spartans imitate?
Or do you mean my tender ears to spare,
That to my questions you so total* are?
When I demand of Phoenix-Stella's state,
You say, forsooth, you left her well of late.
O God, think you that satisfies my care?
I would know whether she did sit or walk;
How cloth'd; how waited on; sigh'd she or smil'd;
Whereof, with whom, how often she did talk;
With what pastime Time's journey she beguil'd;
If her lips deign'd to sweeten my poor name.
Say all, and, all well said, still say the same.

TENTH SONG

O dear life, when shall it be
That mine eyes thine eyes may see?
And in them thy mind discover
Whether absence have had force
Thy remembrance to divorce
From the image of thy lover?

O if I myself find not
After parting aught forgot,
Nor debarr'd from beauty's treasure,
Let no tongue aspire to tell
In what high joys I shall dwell:
Only thought aims at the pleasure.

Thought, therefore, I will send thee
To take up the place for me:
Long I will not after tarry.
There, unseen, thou may'st be bold
Those fair wonders to behold
Which in them my hopes do carry.

Thought, see thou no place forbear,
Enter bravely everywhere;

Seize on all to her belonging.
But if thou would'st guarded be
Fearing her beams, take with thee
Strength of liking, rage of longing.

Think of that most grateful time
When my leaping heart will climb
In my lips to have his biding,
There those roses for to kiss
Which do breathe a sugar'd bliss,
Opening rubies, pearls dividing.

Think of my most princely power
When I blessèd shall devour
With my greedy licorous senses
Beauty, music, sweetness, love,
While she doth against me prove
Her strong darts but weak defences.

Think, think of those dallyings,
When with dovelike murmurings,
With glad moaning, passèd anguish,
We change eyes, and heart for heart
Each to other do depart,
Joying till joy make us languish.

O my thoughts, my thoughts surcease!
Thy delights my woes increase:
My life melts with too much thinking.
Think no more, but die in me,
Till thou shalt revivèd be
At her lips, my nectar drinking.

 93

O fate, O fault, O curse, child of my bliss!
What sobs can give words grace my grief to show?
What ink is black enough to paint my woe?
Through me, wretch me, e'en Stella vexèd is.
Yet, Truth—if caitiff's breath may call thee—this
Witness with me, that my foul stumbling so
From carelessness did in no manner grow,
But wit confus'd with too much care did miss.
And do I, then, myself this vain 'scuse give?
I have—live I, and know this—harmèd thee;
Though worlds 'quite me shall I myself forgive?
Only with pains my pains this easèd be,
That all thy hurts in my heart's wrack I read:
I cry thy sighs, my dear, thy tears I bleed.

94

Grief, find the words, for thou hast made my brain
So dark with misty vapours which arise
From out thy heavy mould, that inbent eyes
Can scarce discern the shape of mine own pain.
Do thou then—for thou canst—do thou complain
For my poor soul, which now that sickness tries
Which e'en to sense sense of itself denies,
Though harbingers of death lodge there his train.
Or if thy love of plaint yet mine forbears,
As of a caitiff worthy so to die,
Yet wail thyself, and wail with causeful tears,
That though in wretchedness thy life doth lie,
Yet growest more wretched than thy nature bears
By being plac'd in such a wretch as I.

Yet sighs, dear sighs, indeed true friends you are,
That do not leave your left friend at the worst,
But as you with my breast I oft have nurs'd,
So, grateful now, you wait upon my care.
Faint coward Joy no longer tarry dare,
Seeing Hope yield when this woe strake him first;
Delight exclaims he is for my fault curs'd,
Though oft himself my mate in arms he sware;
Nay, Sorrow comes with such main rage, that he
Kills his own children, tears, finding that they
By Love were made apt to consort with me.
Only, true sighs, you do not go away;
Thank may you have for such a thankful part,
Thank-worthiest yet when you shall break my heart.

Thought, with good cause thou likest so well the night,
Since kind or chance gives both one livery:
Both sadly black, both blackly darknèd be,
Night barr'd from sun, thou from thy own sunlight.
Silence in both displays his sullen might,
Slow heaviness in both holds one degree,
That full of doubts, thou of perplexity,
Thy tears express Night's native moisture right.
In both amazeful solitariness:
In night, of spirits the ghastly powers do stir,
In thee, or spirits or spirited ghastliness.
But, but, alas, Night's side the odds hath fur,⋆
For that, at length, yet doth invite some rest:
Thou, though still tir'd, yet still dost it detest.

Dian, that fain would cheer her friend the Night,
Shows her oft, at the full, her fairest face,
Bringing with her those starry nymphs, whose chase
From heavenly standing* hits each mortal wight.*
But ah, poor Night, in love with Phoebus' light,
And endlessly despairing of his grace,
Herself, to show no other joy hath place,
Silent and sad in mourning weeds doth dight.*
E'en so, alas, a lady,* Dian's peer,
With choice delights and rarest company
Would fain drive clouds from out my heavy cheer;
But, woe is me, though Joy itself were she,
She could not show my blind brain ways of joy,
While I despair my sun's sight to enjoy.

98

Ah bed! the field where Joy's peace some do see,
The field where all my thoughts to war be train'd,
How is thy grace by my strange fortune stain'd!
How thy lee-shores by my sighs stormèd be!
With sweet soft shades thou oft invitest me
To steal some rest; but, wretch, I am constrain'd—
Spurr'd with Love's spur, though gall'd and shortly rein'd
With Care's hard hand—to turn and toss in thee,
While the black horrors of the silent night
Paint Woe's black face so lively to my sight
That tedious leisure marks each wrinkl'd line.
But when Aurora leads out Phoebus' dance,
Mine eyes then only wink; for spite, perchance,
That worms should have their sun, and I want mine.

When far-spent Night persuades each mortal eye,
To whom nor Art nor Nature granteth light,
To lay his then mark-wanting shafts of sight,
Clos'd with their quivers, in Sleep's armoury,
With windows ope then most my mind doth lie
Viewing the shape of darkness, and delight
Takes on that sad hue which with the inward night
Of his maz'd powers keeps perfect harmony.
But when birds charm, and that sweet air which is
Morn's messenger with rose-enamell'd skies
Calls each wight to salute the flower of bliss,
In tomb of lids then buried are mine eyes,
Forc'd by their lord, who is asham'd to find
Such light in sense with such a darken'd mind.

O tears! no tears, but rain from Beauty's skies,
Making those lilies and those roses grow
Which, aye most fair, now more than most fair show,
While graceful Pity Beauty beautifies.
O honied sighs! which from that breast do rise,
Whose pants do make unspilling cream to flow,
Wing'd with whose breath so pleasing zephyrs blow
As can refresh the hell where my soul fries.
O plaints! conserv'd in such a sugar'd phrase
That Eloquence itself envies your praise,
While sobb'd-out words a perfect music give.
Such tears, sighs, plaints, no sorrow is, but joy;
Or, if such heavenly signs must prove annoy,
All mirth farewell, let me in sorrow live.

Stella *is sick, and in that sick-bed lies*
Sweetness which breathes and pants as oft as she;
And Grace, sick too, such fine conclusion* tries
That Sickness brags itself best grac'd to be.
Beauty is sick, but sick in so fair guise
That in that paleness Beauty's white we see,
And Joy, which is inseparate from those eyes,
Stella, *now learns—strange case—to weep in thee.*
Love moans thy pain, and like a faithful page,
As thy looks stir, runs up and down to make
All folks press'd at thy will thy pain to assuage.
Nature with care sweats for her darling's sake,
Knowing worlds pass ere she enough can find
Of such heaven-stuff to clothe so heavenly a mind.

102

Where be those roses gone which sweeten'd so our eyes?
Where those red cheeks which oft with fair increase did
  frame
The height of honour in the kindly badge of shame?
Who hath the crimson weeds stol'n from my morning
  skies?
How doth the colour vade* of those vermilion dyes,
Which Nature self did make engrain'd the same?
I would know by what right this paleness overcame
That hue whose force my heart still unto thraldom ties?
Galen's* adoptive sons, who by a beaten way
Their judgments hackney* on, the fault of sickness lay;
But feeling proof makes me say they mistake it fur:*
It is but Love which makes this paper perfect white,
To write therein more fresh the story of delight,
Whiles Beauty's reddest ink Venus for him doth stir.

O *happy* Thames *that didst my* Stella *bear,*
I saw thyself with many a smiling line
Upon thy cheerful face Joy's livery wear,
While those fair planets on thy streams did shine.
The boat for joy could not to dance forbear,
While wanton winds, with beauties so divine
Ravish'd, stay'd not till in her golden hair
They did themselves—O sweetest prison—twine.
And fain those Aeol's *youth* there would their stay*
Have made, but forc'd by Nature still to fly,
First did with puffing kiss those locks display:
She, so dishevell'd blush'd; from window I
With sight thereof cried out: 'O fair disgrace,
Let Honour self to thee grant highest place.'

Envious wits, what hath been mine offence
That with such poisonous care my looks you mark,
That to each word, nay sigh of mine, you hark,
As grudging me my sorrow's eloquence?
Ah, is it not enough that I am thence,
Thence, so far thence, that scantly any spark
Of comfort dare come to this dungeon dark,
Where Rigour's exile locks up all my sense?
But if I by a happy window pass,
If I but stars upon mine armour bear,
Sick, thirsty, glad—though but of empty glass—
Your moral notes straight my hid meaning tear
From out my ribs, and puffing proves that I
Do Stella love: fools, who doth it deny?

ELEVENTH SONG

'Who is it that this dark night
Underneath my window plaineth?'
'It is one who from thy sight
Being, ah, exil'd, disdaineth
Every other vulgar light.'

'Why, alas, and are you he?
Be not yet those fancies changèd?'
'Dear, when you find change in me,
Though from me you be estrangèd,
Let my change to ruin be.'

'Well, in absence this will die;
Leave to see and leave to wonder.'
'Absence sure will help, if I
Can learn how myself to sunder
From what in my heart doth lie.'

'But time will these thoughts remove:
Time doth work what no man knoweth.'
'Time doth as the subject prove:
With time still the affection groweth
In the faithful turtle dove.'

'What if you new beauties see,
Will not they stir new affection?'
'I will think they pictures be,
Image-like of saints' perfection,
Poorly counterfeiting thee.'

'But your reason's purest light
Bids you leave such minds to nourish?'
'Dear, do reason no such spite;
Never doth thy beauty flourish
More than in my reason's sight.'

'But the wrongs love bears will make
Love at length leave undertaking.'
'No, the more fools it do shake,
In a ground of so firm making
Deeper still they drive the stake.'

'Peace, I think that some give ear;
Come, no more lest I get anger.'
'Bliss, I will my bliss forbear,
Fearing, sweet, you to endanger;
But my soul shall harbour there.'

'Well, begone, begone I say,
Lest that Argus' eyes perceive you.'
'O unjust is Fortune's sway,
Which can make me thus to leave you,
And from louts to run away.'

Unhappy sight, and hath she vanish'd by
So near, in so good time, so free a place?
Dead glass, dost thou thy object so embrace
As what my heart still sees thou canst not spy?
I swear, by her I love and lack, that I
Was not in fault who bent thy dazzling race
Only unto the heaven of Stella's face,
Counting but dust what in the way did lie.
But cease, mine eyes, your tears do witness well
That you, guiltless thereof, your nectar miss'd.
Curs'd be the page from whom the bad torch fell:
Curs'd be the night which did your strife resist:
Curs'd be the coachman that did drive so fast,
With no worse curse than absence makes me taste.

O absent presence! Stella is not here.
False-flattering hope, that with so fair a face
Bare me in hand,* that in this orphan place
Stella, I say my Stella, should appear.
What say'st thou now? Where is that dainty cheer
Thou told'st mine eyes should help their famish'd
  case?
But thou art gone, now that self-felt disgrace
Doth make me most to wish thy comfort near.
But here I do store of fair ladies meet
Who may with charm of conversation sweet
Make in my heavy mould new thoughts to grow.
Sure they prevail as much with me as he
That bad his friend, but then new-maim'd, to be
Merry with him, and so forget his woe.

107*

Stella, *since thou so right a princess art*
Of all the powers which life bestows on me,
That ere by them aught undertaken be
They first resort unto that sovereign part;
Sweet, for a while give respite to my heart,
Which pants as though it still could leap to thee,
And on my thoughts give thy lieutenancy
To this great cause, which needs both use and art.
And as a queen, who from her presence sends
Whom she employs, dismiss from thee my wit,
Till it have wrought what thy own will attends:
On servants' shame oft master's blame doth sit.
O, let not fools in me thy works reprove,
And scorning say, 'See what it is to love!'

When Sorrow, using mine own fire's might,
Melts down his lead into my boiling breast,
Through that dark furnace to my heart oppress'd
There shines a joy from thee, my only light;
But soon as thought of thee breeds my delight,
And my young soul flutters to thee his nest,
Most rude Despair, my daily unbidden guest,
Clips straight my wings, straight wraps me in his
   night,
And makes me then bow down my head and say:
'Ah, what doth Phoebus' gold that wretch avail
Whom iron doors do keep from use of day?'
So strangely, alas, thy works in me prevail,
That in my woes for thee thou art my joy,
And in my joys for thee my only annoy.

Glossary and Notes

Sonnet

2 *dribbèd shot:* an arrow shot so that it falls short or wide of the mark.
in mine of time: as time passed. (The metaphor contains a reference to the mining operations used in sieges.)
footstep: trace, vestige.

3 *Pindar's apes:* a reference to imitators of Ronsard, and not to imitators in general.
new-found tropes: new figurative language, new styles in poetry.
sprites: spirits.

4 *a bate:* debate, contention.

5 *shade:* reflexion.
country: heaven.

6 *Another humbler wit:* a reference to the poet Spenser.

8 *Love, born in Greece . . . fine-pointed dart:* Cyprus, traditionally held to be the home of Cupid's mother, was captured by the Turks in 1573; the hearts of the Cypriots are here supposed to have been hardened by their conquerors, thus making them unsuitable targets for the arrows of Cupid.
clips: embraces.

9 *touch:* the meaning of the word here is almost lost in a confusion of puns. In these three lines the word has four different meanings: (i) Stella's black eyes are like touchstone, glossy and black; (ii) they have no power to touch in the ordinary physical sense, but (iii) act as a touchstone of beauty to the observer, and as (iv) a touch powder to start a fire.

10 *brabbling:* squabbling, quarrelling noisily.

11 *lookt'st babies:* amorously. To look babies refers to the small images of oneself reflected the pupils of another's eyes.

pitfold: a concealed pit or trap for the unwary, having a diminutive suggestion because the word described a gin or snare for small birds.

bo-peep or couching lies: Cupid is here described as coming to rest in Stella's bosom, either playing the nursery game of bo-peep there or revealing himself clearly to the eye in a position of rest (couching) after having been seen in her eyes and cheeks.

12 *day-nets:* a method of catching birds by attracting them towards pieces of glass placed so as to reflect the sun, then throwing a net over them.

13 *vert:* heraldic green.

gules: heraldic red.

blaze: to blazon is used here in the technical sense of showing arms in their proper colours.

14 *gripe:* vulture. *tire:* tear with the beak.

rhubarb words: words of cleansing bitterness. Rhubarb was supposed to purge the liver, the seat of desire and fleshly love.

15 *Ye that do . . . rattling rows:* Sidney's scornful reference to the methods used by some of his contemporaries to find extravagant alliteration.

denizen'd wit: foreign words and expressions naturalized into the language.

far-fet: far-fetched.

bewray: to reveal oneself involuntarily.

inward touch: inner perception, either moral or mental.

17 *in chafe:* 'in a pet', in irritation.

18 *shent:* punished.

toys: trifles. Sidney referred to his *Arcadia* as 'my toyful book.'

20 *fair level:* good aim. *secret stay:* hidden ambush.

21 *windlass:* ensnare circuitously or craftily.

coltish gyres: a reference to the *Phaedrus*, where Socrates speaks of the struggles of the soul to control the horses by which its chariot is drawn.

22 *fair Twin's:* in the first fortnight of June, when the sun is passing from Gemini to Cancer.

23 *bewray:* reveal itself involuntarily.

24 *Rich:* The first of the sonnets in which Sidney plays on the name of Lord Rich, Stella's husband.
Tantal's smart: Tantalus, mythical king of Phrygia, and son of Zeus, was condemned to stand in Tartarus up to his chin in water for betraying the secrets of the gods. The water receded when he tried to drink, and the fruit above his head always evaded his grasp.

25 *Phoebus' doom:* the judgment of the oracle of Apollo at Delphi. The oracle declared that Socrates was the wisest of men (*of the wight most wise*); his wisest scholar is Plato, and the reference here is to Plato speaking of virtue in the *Phaedrus*.

26 *braule:* a kind of cotillion of French origin.

27 *doom:* judgment.

28 *slake:* slack.

30 The historical events referred to would seem to place this sonnet early in 1581. A Turkish campaign was expected (ll. 1, 2). Henry of Valois had left the throne of Poland for France, and the Polish nobles had elected Stephen Bathori in 1575. In 1581 he had retreated from an unsuccessful campaign against Russia, with the intention of repeating it (ll. 3, 4). The election of Stephen had been much contested, hence Sidney's insistence on *right king*. (There seems little doubt that Sidney himself was offered the throne of Poland.)
The disagreements between Catholics, Protestants and 'politiques' in France (l. 5). Reference to events in Holland in 1581 (ll. 6-8): the Dutch States could not agree to accept the sovereignty of the Duke of Anjou, although the Prince of Orange was in favour of it. The Hollanders would not accept any other governor than the Prince of Orange, and the states were divided into two friendly confederations with Anjou at the head of one.

weltring: vacillation. The editor of the 1598 edition altered this to read 'no weltring', an understandably diplomatic gesture to James VI, whereas in 1581 the notorious vacillation of the Scottish Court would have been a more justifiable comment.

34 *perhaps . . . my mind:* 'although I am so confused, perhaps others will understand'.

35 *Nestor's counsel:* Nestor was a Homeric hero, famous for his age and wisdom. A common allusion in poetry to suggest 'a wise old man'.

37 This sonnet appeared for the first time in the Folio of 1598. It had doubtless been excluded from the earlier editions because of its transparent references to Stella's husband, Lord Rich. (See Introduction.)
Towards Aurora's Court: towards the east, and almost certainly Sidney means more explicitly, Essex. Stella's mother, the Countess of Leicester lived at Wanstead, and Lord Rich's estates were in the same county.

38 *hatch:* close.
unbitted: unrestrained, unbridled.
call'd it anew: refers back to 'Stella's image' in l. 6.

39 *prease:* press.

41 The whole sonnet probably refers to the tilts given in London in the summer of 1581 to entertain the French commissioners, who had come to negotiate the marriage of Elizabeth and the Duke of Anjou.
Of both sides I do take my blood . . .: Sidney had ancestors on both sides of his family who had distinguished themselves in the tilt-yard.

42 *Keep still my zenith:* remain fixed above me.

45 *skill:* an impersonal form, 'it skills not'—it makes no difference, here used personally—'Stella cannot be bothered to pity me.'
Alas, if fancy, etc.: It would be a pity if fiction produced by the free workings of the imagination had more effect on you than the

true story of my ruin, which involves the further complication between love and honour.

46 *myche:* play truant. The sense here is: 'you must forgive the lover's lapses into desire.'

49 *Manège:* display of skilled horsemanship.

50 *put out:* cancel.

51 *silly:* innocent.

54 *pies:* magpies.

58 *lin'd:* backed, supported.
wrate: wrote.
Maugre: in spite of.

59 *clips:* embraces.

FIRST SONG *staineth:* the normal Elizabethan meaning of the verb was 'to take the shine out of'.

65 *prize:* estimate the worth of.
arrow-head: a reference to Sidney's arms, which were argent, a pheon (or arrow head) azure.

66 *stilts:* crutches.

67 *take time:* act in time, *cf.* 'take time by the forelock'.
wrackèd: ruined, destroyed.

74 *Aganippe well:* One of the springs on Mt. Helicon, sacred to the Muses.
Tempe: a valley in classical Sicily, much celebrated by the poets.

75 Edward IV became king at the age of nineteen, avenging his father's death (ll. 5, 6.) Later he resisted the power of the Neville family, at one time the main supporters of his party (ll. 7, 8.) He invaded France and extracted an annual subvention from Louis XI (ll. 9-11.) It is supposed that the main cause of the disagreement with the Nevilles was his marriage to Elizabeth Woodville—which might well have lost him his crown (l. 14).

Sonnet

imp feathers: to graft feathers onto the wing of a bird to improve its flight.

76 *walking head:* it is difficult to determine the exact meaning of this phrase; *walking* may contain a suggestion of one early meaning, 'throbbing' or 'agitated movement', such as can be seen in the flanks of a horse when standing still; it could also mean a lowering of the head towards the ground, as in 'walking plant', a reading which would fit the idea of prayer in the following line.

77 *conster'd:* construed, probably in the sense of 'to combine words grammatically.'

79 *consort:* concert.

80 *stall:* seat of dignity.
resty: restive, in the sense that a horse stubbornly refuses to advance.

81 *shade out:* to sketch faintly.

83 *Good brother Philip:* this sonnet is inspired by the *Boke of Philipp Sparowe*, a poem by John Skelton on the death of a sparrow belonging to Jane Scroupe.
your cut to keep: from Skelton's poem this would seem to mean 'to behave' in the sense of standing to attention, but Sidney may equally be using it in the sense of 'to be on guard' or 'to be on the defensive'. Both meanings could be incorporated here, giving ll. 2-4 this meaning: 'you cunningly assumed a cautious attitude, pretending not to like it when Stella made you stand at attention, thus getting extra petting.'

84 & 85 It is probable that Sidney was riding to the Countess of Leicester's house at Wanstead to see Stella. The highway in Sonnet 84 would then be the Whitechapel Road. Sonnet 85 sees him approaching the house, and the action of the songs that follow would probably refer to the same visit.

85 *The globe of weal:* the total sum of all happiness and delight.

FIFTH SONG *babies:* dolls.
appeach: impeach.
runaway: apostate.

SIXTH SONG *whether:* which, and in verse 9, l. 5.
    bate: debate, controversy.
    Both in . . . touch: Their reliability as witnesses cannot be questioned.
    common sense: a technical term of Aristotelian philosophy, defined by Sidney's friend Bryskett as 'a faculty of the sensitive soul and therefore called because it commonly receives the forms or images which the exterior senses present unto it and distinguishes the one from the other.'

SEVENTH SONG *Whose senses . . . do not raise:* The senses here are likened to a group of instruments (consort) playing out of tune.

EIGHTH SONG *effects:* affectations. 'Do not try to test my love by this display of passion.'

NINTH SONG *blaying:* bleating.

88 *earthly cates:* choice food in the material sense as opposed to the spiritual food mentioned in the preceding line.

90 *laud:* praise, high commendation.

91 *jets black:* black eyes.

92 *cutted:* concise, using short sentences.
    total: used as an adjective; it has somewhat the same meaning as the modern 'summary', or 'brief'.

96 *fur:* by far.

97 *standing:* a station from which to shoot game.
    mortal wight: human being.
    dight: clothe.
    a lady: almost certainly the Countess of Pembroke.

101 *conclusions:* experiments.

102 *vade:* there is a suggestion here of a double meaning; fade, but also associated with the latin *vadere*—disappear, vanish, decay.
    Galen: Claudius Galenus, a celebrated physician of the second century, A.D., who wrote 500 medical treatises, of which 80 have

survived. He was associated with vegetable rather than mineral remedies.

hackney: amble, plod.

103 *Aeol's youth:* Aeolus was the mythical god of the winds. His 'youth' are the *wanton winds* referred to in line 6. It has been suggested that the picture in Sidney's mind might have been inspired by Botticelli's 'Venus', which he may have seen in Florence in 1574.

106 *Bare me in hand:* encouraged me to hope.

107 It seems unlikely that this sonnet refers to Sidney's appointment to the governorship of Flushing, as that would mean that he went on writing sonnets to Stella after his own marriage to Frances Walsingham. It has been suggested that it might refer to an arrangement discussed in 1582, according to which Sidney's father was to return to Ireland as Lord Lieutenant with Sidney himself as his successor.

Index of First Lines